Prepper Pyramid

Frank Harrison

ISBN 978-1625121073

Table of Contents

Prepping for Parents with Adult Children

By

Susan Abercrombie

"Most people don't believe something can happen until it already has. That's not stupidity or weakness, that's just human nature"

World War Z by Max Brooks

When asked to write this portion of *Prepper Pyramid* from the perspective of an older (not that much older but older), married couple with grown children, we thought to ourselves, what could we possibly write about being a Prepper that would take up any more than two or three sentences? To be quite honest, we did not know that there was a name for "people like us".

For us, beginning to become a Prepper began some months before we were asked to write about our thoughts, feelings and actions having to do with how we have been, are and will be preparing for being "prepared". It is just that at the time, we really were not aware of being part of an elite club, if you will. Synchronicity occurs in this universe all the time if you listen and watch and are open to its language. And we do believe that it was beautiful synchronicity that brought certain people and events into our lives at this time to make us aware of some possibilities that we had not thought about before as solidly and with such clarity as we do now. It is only through kindness and love that people share their knowledge in the hope to help others as well as themselves. So we agreed to the honor and privilege of being part of these pages of feelings and knowledge in hopes of entertaining you with just a really good book and hopefully teaching and helping you also.

So when we actually started to put our thoughts on paper, the words flowed easily. We have to think that it is because these types of thoughts are abundant in us concerning this particular subject. Not constant, not obsessive, but abundant. To us being a Prepper is not about being a pessimist or a worrier. It is not about being like poor, little Chicken Little running around screaming that the sky is falling. It is about being a realist. We are not thinking or writing in terms of necessarily a full blown doomsday or apocalypse, but more like a "just in case" if you will. We do not want to find ourselves in a situation like the one that resembles what happens just hours before the storm is about to hit where good folks scramble out to get bread and milk (and probably chocolate). We do think that there have been "doomsday" or "end of the world" theories and stories since humans were in population. We also know that other than events like the Ice Age or Plate shifting, that nothing has really ever happened to actually change the world the way we know it. Admittedly, we have gotten the blank stares and the rolling of eyes when we bring up the subject with some folk.

So what does being a Prepper mean to us?

Being a Prepper encompasses a huge arena of events, situations and thoughts about preparations. To tell the truth, it truly has been and is absolutely, positively, totally fun! And also, it has stretched into our lives to the extent of having become almost a hobby and a way of life.

This is the underlying theme for living a Prepper's life. Living with a certain level of preparedness which will give you the ability to discern and judge, the ability to formulate with complete lucidity and saneness, just how ready you are and how you will approach as many given circumstance which might require drastic measures. Knowing this before the possible tragic event takes place is the very essence of being a Prepper. Waiting and scrambling in a nervous, possibly even paranoid state of being will help no one. Quite possibly there will be no resources with which to scramble to! Being a Prepper means having a plan. A solid, written and mental plan enlisted and ready to be enacted upon no matter how small and benign the event may be or how monstrous and disastrous.

There can be little to no room for surprises or bewilderment on our end. There will be plenty of unforeseen and unexpected issues with the supposed event.

Be it a gas shortage or an ice storm or even just a simple power outage (is there such a thing as a "simple" power outage?). One must stop and think….what would we do? What would be instantly eliminated from our lives should something like this happen? What can we do *now* to make sure that we will not become debilitated with whatever is eliminated from our lives. It is a very difficult notion to wrap our heads around…the fact that everyday goods, gear, just plain stuff will not be available! We are human beings, we have the ability to think and plan and be prepared! We can be Preppers!!

We are from the nineteen sixties. The sixties and seventies were a time that had a certain flare for conspiracy theories. The transition that this era was bringing to our country also brought with it a certain sensation of paranoia. The pop culture of the day seemed to think in terms that the powerful ones were secretly plotting and scheming for the ultimate demise of the American people. Everywhere you turned, the plots of conspiracy were there. So we, having been from this era, have seen and heard our share of conspiracy theories. Theories not necessarily having to do with the end of the world as we know it and not nearly as technological and advanced as those we are faced with today. Some were just silly, possibly based in fac,t but silly nonetheless and some were of substance, or at least what seemed of substance at that point in time. When we stop and think of a few, it makes us giggle but wonder at the same time.

Please allow us to share just a few with you. The supposed moon landing hoax is one that comes to mind. There were several media presentations depicting just how the landing could have been recreated here on earth. The inconsistencies and discrepancies in the photographs were splattered all over magazines and television specials. "How could this be"? We asked in shock. Have we been deceived? We remember very well being told that there was subliminal advertising being fed to us during Television shows. Depending on just how persuasive the message that was being delivered was, we would be persuaded to do any number of things such as eat at this fast food restaurant or buy this particular product. We scanned and scoured each television show for these horrific messages that were eventually going to Zombify us. And some of us swore that we were able to peak a glance of said message. True terror.

And, of course, if you slowed down your Long Playing records that you were playing on the turnstile, Satanic words could be heard…Devil, Devil! You are Satan!! In this manner, was the general thought of the day, we would eventually all become Satanists and the deed would be taken care of. These all seem pretty tame but at the time, our minds were aghast with the possibility of any such occurrences could be taking place! It was a horrible thought to even remotely think that our upstanding government would do or allow such things to take place. We were definitely a wee bit naïve.

Then, of course, there was surveillance and espionage…Big Brother watching our every move. Classifying in a Matrix-ish manner our every step in hopes to…this we never found out. We remember distinctly not wanting to drink the water because people were saying that there was LSD in it!!! They said that Lee Harvey Oswald did not act alone, that it was, in fact, a government conspiracy. Or was it that Lee Harvey Oswald put the LSD in the water?

On a more contemporary note, why does the Food and Drug Administration allow the increasing use of high fructose corn syrup in our foods? Is it to promote obesity? To then promote the use of medical facilities? Who can trace our whereabouts through our Global Positioning Systems in our fancy phones? Are we all under complete surveillance like the good people in Orwell's *1984*? And of course why did Princess Diana have to die? Camille was already in the picture, wasn't she?

Tragic as it was, September 11, 2001 had a host of conspiracy theories trailing it. Some were incredibly plausible. The latest theory that we have heard and the most unfathomable conspiracy theory that we could ever imagine, is the one surrounding the killing of twenty children and six adults on December 14, 2012 at the Sandy Hook Elementary School in Connecticut. This event, supposedly having been staged to further empower Federal government to confiscate our firearms is tragic enough without an unthinkable plot behind it.

I'm sure there were many, many more that we have not listed. But these theories are more related to events and situations and people bunking or debunking these events and situations. These are the types of theories you can take and believe or you can leave them alone. You just have to be aware by doing your homework and research and either buy into them or leave them alone. For example, just because our foods are processed to the hilt and high fructose corn syrup is in almost all of the processed foods in our grocery stores, we do not have to buy them. We can choose to stay healthier and not let the huge pharmaceutical companies and medical facilities run our lives in the form of over examinations, testing and medications while they get even huger on our dollars.

We can go beyond what is being force is fed into mainstream America. We can choose to make our own decisions based on factual research of our own. We can choose to take care of ourselves and not relay on the forces that be.

A Prepper, if you will, does the same. A Prepper takes care of himself and rises above the lies and the cover-ups. We can see through it and refuse to be led along like herds of cattle, like the masses. We do our homework and research. We talk with fellow Preppers and we share and learn.

So now, now we are faced with new theories and possibilities that seem to have taken on a much grander scale in terms of just how many people on this earth could be affected and in what ways we could be affected. What actually would be the effect on us as a species, animals, plant life and our world? We do not really know. We can surmise and speculate however, and use those thoughts to help us prepare, to help us be Preppers.

"There will be signs in the sun, the moon, and the stars, and on earth nations will be in dismay, perplexed by the roaring of the sea and the waves" Luke 21:25-26 KJV

The end as we know it or the apocalypse, as we have come to coin it, according to Wikipedia actually means… " 'un-covering', translated literally from Greek, is a disclosure of knowledge, hidden from humanity in an era dominated by falsehood and misconception, i.e., a lifting of the veil or revelation…". This sounds much softer than the street definition of apocalypse which we have always heard and understood to be more to the effect of horrific heat, gnashing of teeth, screams of terror, fire and brimstone (or really just the odor of sulfur). Maybe, however, the message in Wiki's definition is just that…a lifting of the veil of ignorance. The ignorance of thinking that "they" say everything is just ducky. "They" say that we will be just fine because "they" will take care of us. Are we as Preppers ready to uncover the lies and deceptions that have been forced upon us, the veils of possibilities and untruths and disclose to ourselves the awareness of knowing that we can and do have to power to be prepared? We think so. We really do.

"And I saw a new heaven and a new earth for the first heaven and the first earth were passed away: and there was no more sea". Revelations 21"1 KJV

Why we as a race are so consumed with the end of this world as we know it is quite understandable. Throughout history, the end, the apocalypse has been a huge component of many myths, stories and religions. To name just a few, about 2800 BC, Assyrian clay tablets wrote of …"Our earth is degenerate in these latter days. There are signs that the world is speedily coming to an end"… Isaac Asimov's Book of Facts (1979).* Lotharingian computists foresaw the End on Friday, March 25, 970. (Source: Center for Millennial Studies [www.mille.org/scholarship/1000/ahr9.html]). * 1862, The end of 6000 years since Creation, and thus the end of the world, according to John Cumming of the Scottish National Church. *End Times Visions*, NY 1998 Abanes p.283.* 1910, The end of the world according to Jehovah's Witnesses. *The Last Days are Here Again*. Baker Books, Grand Rapids MI, 1998. Kyle, p 93.* 1983, Apocalyptic war between the US and the Soviet Union was supposed to break out by the end of 1983, said the *End Times News Digest*. * 1999, The Branch Davidians believed that David Koresh would return to Earth on this day, 2300 days (Daniel 8:14) after his death. (Source: Ontario Consultants on Religious Tolerance [www.religioustolerence.org/dc_branc.htm]). * 1-1-2000 Y2K!!!!! December 2012, the supposed end of the Mayan Calendar and the end of the world as we know it…

Not to mention the outrageously long list of contemporary apocalyptic books and movies describing how our species will become zombie-like, cannibalistic and deranged.

How ironic is that? No sooner did we become a thinking, communicating species then did we start to prepare for the end! We often wonder if our brains are hardwired to think in such a manner. It seems that this way of thinking would fall under some kind of a primitive type survival instinct…Survival being the key word. Survivalist is synonymous with Prepper but Prepper is just so catchy!

*http://www.abhota.info/end1.htm

What is frightening to us about all this end talk, however, is that since much of our society has become consumed with an apocalyptic possibility of global annihilation, will we actually make it a reality? Will we be the ones ultimately responsible for the formation of something so horrific and so terrible? A catastrophic crisis situation that would not have taken place but did, simply because it was so in the forefront of our thoughts?

We are firm believers in the idea that thoughts are things. That if given enough thought on one matter, in this case, some sort of an end of life as we know it occurrence, that eventually that very thought will become a reality. If we were all to think, instead, in terms of global peace and purposeful harmony among the countries and the universe, we firmly believe that this is how it would play out. We as Preppers have a responsibility to ourselves and to the universe to shift our thinking away from the possible cataclysmic event. We need to tip the scale and flip the see-saw from making the thoughts of annihilation heavier than the thoughts of preparation. Perhaps if collectively we shift our thoughts to be not so much on the possible horrific episode but on only the preparation for such an occurrence, we can eliminate the eminent doom thoughts and there-fore, quite possibly, the eminent doom…

Having said that….as we sit in our well lit room, with the soft heat purring and keeping us warm, drinking a hot cup of tea, we wonder…. What if….just what if the computers that we are using were to not function, nor the lights in the room. No hot water for our tea. No heat in this house in the middle of January or for that matter no air conditioning in the Deep South in the middle of August? We could not have taken the shower that we just took or the interim cleansing. There would be no soft music playing in the background. No stove top for us to cook this evening's meal. No mode of communication, restricted means of cooking, no running water. No gasoline for our vehicles, if they were to even function. The list of have nots could go on and on and on.

Our bodies would begin to stink, our bellies would growl, our throats would thirst and all of the creature comforts that we have gotten to know so well would cease. Simply cease. Would that thin veneer that is loosely adhered to us which we call "Being Civilized" vanish very quickly? Would we become as the movies portray us….cannibals, deranged, animal like? Would our human race become blind with terror? Became seething with anger to the point where we were pulling guns on each other in gas lines, as was the case directly after Hurricane Sandy in 2012 ?

When we think of what could happen our blood runs cold.

"What's going to happen is, very soon, we're going to run out of petroleum, and everything de-pends on petroleum. And there go the school buses. There go the fire engines. The food trucks will come to a halt. This is the end of the world."

Kurt Vonnegut, Jr. Rolling Stone, August 24, 2006

The "we" that we have been referring to all along in this writing are my husband and myself. We are what they, (they being societal clichés), call… empty nesters. Yes, we were born in the nine-teen fifties and nineteen sixties.. We are baby boomers and the love product of depression born parents. Will there ever be a generation that witnessed so very many wars and hardships as did they? Let us seriously hope not. But they, having been depression born people, kept house and raised their families in a very different way than most folk have since them. Both of us saw how frugally our parents lived. Nothing was wasted and nothing was thrown out without finding at least ten more uses for it. Name brands were of no use and our wardrobes were extremely slight. Food was NEVER thrown out, but recycled into a vast array of leftovers. And it must have been Saturday if there was a special dessert. There were no trips to "the Mall" just for the sake of shopping. If you needed it, and they had the money, then you got it. If not, you just made due without it.

Because of the way we were raised, unconsciously, or maybe consciously, we have always approached "modern" life in a very old fashioned way. We have always hung linens out to dry thereby saving electricity. Reusing paper and plastic bags and paper towels is a must. Keeping the heat at a lower temperature or the air conditioning at a higher temperature and supplementing with more clothing or less is a priority. Sewing holes in socks or panties instead of throwing them out is always fun. And then, and only when they have rendered themselves useless for their task, they become rags. When we cook, we always make a little more for the freezer. If an appliance or car or some household item breaks in some fashion, we try effortlessly to fix it ourselves before spending money to fix it. Coupon usage is a must. Second hand clothes are real easy on the pocketbook and bartering is just plain fun. Now, are we saying that we do not take part in the conveniences of life? Absolutely not what we are saying at all. We enjoy as much as we can. But these actions of ours are presented to you to better understand who we are, how we were raised and how that has affected our way of life. A way of life that we think and hope more and more folks are returning to.

Today, we live in such a throwaway society because the thought has been inbred into us that we used it, we throw it out and we can just go out and buy another one. This is a mind frame that can*not* be that of a Prepper. We all need to recognize the waste and be dutiful in rethinking just how we can accustom ourselves into reusing and finding new uses for our goods. Should there be a crisis situation, this frugal and creative way of thinking will be crucial. Truth of the matter is that many of us, like my husband and myself, when you really think about it, have always been Preppers to a certain extent, we just did not have a nifty moniker!

So here we are, my husband and I married for twenty eight years. We have birthed and bred three beautiful children. Somehow the time flew by while moving and living all over this great country. We always knew in our logical minds that of course the children would grow up and have lives of their own. But we thought for some reason, and we hoped in our hearts, that our situation was different. That we would always have children around us even though we were watching and experiencing them growing before our very eyes! We watched the infant become a toddler and the toddler a young child. The adolescent followed all too quickly and the teenager appeared what seemed like overnight. But still, life always teasingly hinted that it would just continue in that way; that our children would just be there. Obviously, our thoughts of perpetual children around the home and hearth did not transpire. We are now alone to enjoy our marriage, relationship, home and each other.

It may seem that because our children are self-sufficient and living on their own that the thought of a crisis happening, in terms of us thinking about and worrying about our children, would be less severe than perhaps couples with small children living at home. But in actuality, in the event of a widespread disaster, the idea of our children being so far away from us and scattered in different states is heart wrenching. The possibility being very real that we would never see them again or at least not see them for a very long time is unbearable. Knowing that we have prepared as much as we can for our own survival and not being able to share that with our offspring is a horribly revolting thought. We have spoken to them about being a Prepper and they have acknowledged sincerely that they would like to be somewhat prepared, but sheer acknowledgment is not enough. We know that they might not have the funds to indulge in Prepping. We know that they do not have the room to store items. And we know that the cities that they live in are huge with very little rural escapes. It is these types of cities where one imagines true civil unrest would occur. Given these circumstances, it's easy to see why we would rather have our children all living close to us in the event of a catastrophe, but that scenario, for us at this juncture, is practically an impossibility. Are we saying that it is easier to have small children living with you so that you can work together and survive together? No, not at all. It is true, however, that on the flip side, we do not have to have a cache of supplies which includes diapers, formula, ointments and the whole host of baby supplies!

But, here is the very fabric of being a Prepper at *this* point in life, at *our* point in life. Yes, our grown children are settled in their lives and have their partners and are very happy but it is excruciatingly painful to know that we are taking so many precautions and preparing in so many ways and cannot or probably will not be able to share this with our children. It is the duty of a parent to keep their children safe and far from harms way, so the thought of possibly not being able to do that is just awful for both of us.. We take solace, however, in knowing that perhaps if we cannot help our own children that we can help others and that hopefully others will help our children should a harmful event or situation occur.

The following are the types of events or situations that we have read about and heard say that will, might, could, probably will not and even bound to happen. Are these, in fact, what might be in store for us?

Electromagnetic pulse, from either a nuclear weapon or a solar flare would create extensive damaging effects on our power lines and electrical equipment. The electrical grid would cease. Cities will darken and silence will loom until the shock is over and the civil unrest begins. Life as we once knew it will end. And there not only is the possibility but the probability of a collapse of a civilization.

The "Double Punch", terrorist deployed nuclear weapons which causes an electromagnetic pulse that destroys the electrical grids; all the equipment is then removed from Faraday Cages and bam another EMP to completely debilitate us and the equipment that we salvaged.

Economic collapse, which would lead to a societal collapse with the dollar worth practically nothing. Only the coins would be worth whatever their content, be it nickel or silver or even gold.

Expansion of the sun causing extremely high temperatures which would evaporate water, kill crops and eventually bring death to all.

Effects of a polar shift involving the wobbling of the earth, and a change in pole location with respect to the crust and core would result in dramatic changes to the topography of the earth along with grand destruction from earthquakes and tsunamis.

A polar shift if caused by a massive asteroid or collision with a rogue planet would cause damage that is beyond our scope of imagination.

WWIII, no explanation needed here.

Christian Rapture day by using biblical calculations. The ever looming second coming for all to be judged...Judgment day.

Epidemics, pandemics caused by overuse of antibiotics., The slow eruption of super viral and bacterial strains.

Alignment of planets causing a severe black out. Depending on how long this remained, a gradual freeze would kill all.

The effects of bee colony collapse caused by overuse of pesticides would halt the pollination of agricultural crops for food consumption and also plants in the wild would stop being pollinated resulting in world famine.

Overuse of stronger and stronger pesticides used in farming compromising our health and resulting in super weeds unable to be stopped unless yet stronger pesticides are produced. Vicious circle...

Super volcanoes and/or super earthquakes.

Terrorist acts that do not involve nuclear weapons but still cause mass destruction.

Reduction or complete end to the world's crude oil and fuel reserve. Hopefully we will have created alternate resources before the crude oil runs out. Nuclear, solar, wind and hydroelectric power will become more prevalent. Our vehicles would have to become hybrids of some sort.

Gravitational shifts, do not really know the difference between these and polar shifts but we have heard of it.

Overpopulation resulting in world famine.

Global warming causing environmental collapse.

Total pollution of the earth's water supply due to either our own misuse or a terrorist act.

Not so fun to think about but definitely necessary to be aware of. We as Preppers see and understand the potential gravity of the outcome of any of these situations and surely others that were not mentioned. The time to act and get ready is now.

For us, and probably for all of you, an electromagnetic pulse sent via a terrorist country or a solar flare or caused by any other trigger, either natural or man-made is the most frightening. The thought of losing nationwide electrical grids for months or even years is beyond our scope of our imagination. Life would return as it was hundreds of years ago. Given the level that we are able to communicate with each other at this point in time, the change from going from being ultra-plugged in by phone, smartphone, Facebook®, Facetime®, Twitter®, Shutterfly®, Blogs, Internet, and even postal service would simply cease! This is paramount to what we mean when we say that it is a horrific thought when we imagine the fact that we might not be able to communicate with our grown children who do not live close to us should this become a reality.

We must, however horrific to think about, run this through logically and be as prepared as humanly possible. Being a Prepper and being prepared in a grid down event, will quite literally make the difference between life and death. There are those who would argue to the point of why would anyone even want to survive such an event and quite possibly live in horrific conditions. This is an argument to make but it is each and everyone's choice to make. We have chosen to be prepared as much as possible.

The following is a list of items which we have procured or are procuring which we think will help us to reach a level of Prepper preparedness comparable with our particular plan:

FOOD

☐ Canned: separated by expiration date which we have marked on top and bottom of can

☐ Jarred

☐ Frozen

☐ Dried

☐ Heirloom seeds and ongoing compost for our garden

☐ Coffee

☐ Alcohol for consumption

☐ Chickens for eggs, if you can keep them

☐ Candies

☐ Garden

☐ Root cellar

WATER

☐ Bottled; separated by expiration date

☐ Empty, clean bottles for rainwater collection

☐ Empty, clean rainwater collection barrels

☐ Water purifier

ENERGY

- [ ] 1800 Solar Power System: tested but not deployed and in Faraday Cage
- [ ] Generators; at least one in a Faraday Cage
- [ ] Gasoline in containers with additives for long term storage and/or rotate stored gasoline into automobile and keep fresh in container
- [ ] Propane in small containers and large
- [ ] Batteries of assorted types with some wrapped in aluminum foil
- [ ] Rechargeable batteries with solar recharge
- [ ] Wood burning stove
- [ ] Firewood
- [ ] Non electric emergency pump for emptying swimming pool

SELF DEFENSE AND HUNTING

- [ ] Guns: shotgun, handgun, rifle, sling shot with gathered rocks or shots, bow and arrow
- [ ] Scope: preferably for a .22 Rifle for shooting small animals for food
- [ ] Plenty of ammunition for all guns in household: at least 1,000 rounds per gun.
- [ ] Hunting knives
- [ ] Pepper spray

COMMUNICATION

- [ ] Radios in Faraday Boxes: at least one with a hand crank
- [ ] Ham radio
- [ ] CB radio
- [ ] Walkie Talkies
- [ ] Rechargeable batteries for above with solar recharger

LOCOMOTION

- [ ] All terrain-vehicle
- [ ] Mini bike
- [ ] Car/Trucks
- [ ] Bicycles

TOILETRIES

- [ ] Feminine products
- [ ] Toilet paper
- [ ] Wipees
- [ ] Kleenex
- [ ] Alcohol for antiseptic
- [ ] Antiseptic creams
- [ ] Soap
- [ ] Bandages and Band aides
- [ ] Antibiotics if possible
- [ ] Ibuprofen
- [ ] Cold and Flu meds
- [ ] Toothpaste, tooth powder and tooth brushes
- [ ] Watch expiration dates and rotate as used

EQUIPMENT

- [ ] Optical Discs with computer file backups
- [ ] Flashlights with rechargeable batteries and solar recharger
- [ ] Candles
- [ ] Lighters
- [ ] Matches: Strike Anywhere
- [ ] Can openers: hand operated
- [ ] Camping type equipment like lanterns, sleeping bags, solar blankets
- [ ] Propane stove with fittings for different sized tanks
- [ ] Old fashioned, stove top percolator
- [ ] Blankets: regular and solar
- [ ] Hand tools: axe, pliers, hammer, screwdrivers, Swiss-knife
- [ ] Fishing pole/accessories
- [ ] Faraday Cages

MISCELLANEOUS

- [ ] Bleach

- ☐ Rubber bands
- ☐ Bungee cords
- ☐ Plastic and paper bags
- ☐ Clean rags
- ☐ Aluminum foil
- ☐ Twine and Para cord
- ☐ Blankets: regular and solar
- ☐ Sturdy shoes and boots: preferably multiple pairs
- ☐ Cigarettes if you smoke
- ☐ Musical instruments and board games to keep our spirits up
- ☐ Money in small bills and coins
- ☐ Duct tape

OUR BASIC HOUSE RULES ON A REAL MINIMAL LEVEL

- ☐ Never let gasoline levels in vehicles get below the half mark.
- ☐ Always keep vehicle mechanicals up to date.
- ☐ Keep 3 flats of bottled drinking water at all times…use one, replace one.
- ☐ Have some frozen, purchased or pre-cooked meals in your freezer.
- ☐ Make sure that house mechanicals are always in order.
- ☐ Always have flashlights ready with fresh batteries
- ☐ Have at the very least one week's worth of canned/jarred food.
- ☐ Have an emergency plan in place for how to face the event.
- ☐ Have a rendezvous point and know the means by which to get there.
- ☐ Have a backpack in your vehicle with bottled water, jacket, scarf, socks, energy bars, pepper spray and small knife, aka "Bug-Out Bag"

We think it is safe to say that about fifty percent of people in any situation, even if not consciously Preppers, are likely to be prepared at this minimum level having covered the basic rules. Most homes have a couple of days' worth of food in the pantry, some frozen goods that would last a few days in the freezer, and some fresh food in the refrigerator. Water could still be an issue, but drinkable liquids such as soda, electrolyte water and some bottled water would probably prevail in most people's fridge. At the very minimum, we hope that this is the case. Quite honestly, there is no excuse for not being prepared at this minimal level given all that we have witnessed and have heard about in terms of potential threats.

FOOD AND WATER

As far as the gathering of provisions and the accumulation of any one item, the procurement of food and water is at the top of the list. We have used the Food Storage Chart found in Appendix A at the back of this book to help decide which foods would keep better and where to focus our purchases. The Food and Non-Food Inventory sheets, Appendix D, also found at the end of this book, are great to keep track of what you have in stock, dates of their expiration, and if you should use an item due to its being close to expiration, keeping a log with the Storage Chart helps to ensure that you will then replace it. Again, food and water collection, we think, is imperative but having the room to store it can be tricky. We have gotten pretty creative in terms of finding space for storage.

At the Minimal and Basic Pyramid Level, we would use up all frozen and refrigerated food first so as to prevent spoilage and waste. Rations would be decided and adhered to. Water and coffee would be rationed too even at the Minimal level. Should the crisis continue and the Prepper Pyramid time clock move to the Robust, Extreme and Off the Grid levels, hopefully we would have purchased enough food and water to last us a year if need be.

We currently have a 12 gauge shotgun for bird and deer hunting (with Slugs); and a .22 rifle for rabbit and squirrel hunting. Hunting as a hobby is an ongoing process, but in a catastrophic situation, depending on the food supplies on hand, hunting for nutritional survival will have to come into play. So when our cache of frozen food dwindled, we would hunt and fish for sustenance thus preserving most of our canned and dry food until the expiration date. We find ourselves fortunate to live out in a more rural area of the country. We have a 10 acre property which is set back from the main road by about 1,700 feet with one access driveway. The entire property is surrounded with barbed wire fencing and very thick forest. Although somewhat in the distance, we have kind and like-minded neighbors. There is a fresh water stream which runs through our property all year long and wild berries, wild onions and many persimmon trees grow. A home setting like ours really is ideal in an Off the Grid situation. At the Robust, Extreme and Off the Grid levels, if we have run out of water, thankfully we would have set out the rainwater barrels and use the Water Purifier for both the creek water and the collected rainwater. Just a note, make sure if you purchase a water purifier that you try it out first!

We are heartened to know that in our county, virtually everyone who lives here knows how to fish and hunt and have a general knowledge of living off the land. We do not want to sound selfish but given that this is the case, there is little fear that our neighbors will be the ones knocking down our doors for supplies. We would, however share if asked.

We also plant a yearly garden and for the sake of now being Preppers, we have purchased Heirloom seeds and seed potatoes in hopes of being able to re-plant, gather and store the more sturdy vegetables in our root cellar. Not so popular now except in the more rural areas, root cellars are invaluable when refrigeration is no longer possible. In a grid down situation, having had stored vegetable, fruits and even some cured meats in a root cellar could make the difference between starving or not. In older times, consumable alcohol was kept in the root cellars also. Not a bad idea!

We also keep <u>chickens</u> for eggs which comes in very handy. Since we would probably not have stocked too much chicken feed, we would let them graze for food all day. As heartless as it sounds, once the laying of eggs stopped, roast chicken would be dinner.

ENERGY

Energy, from a Preppers perspective, to us is next in the line of importance. Having accumulated as much as possible in as many forms as possible before a situation is paramount. We are betting that one of the first items to disappear from the shelves in the aftermath of a disaster (along with milk and bread) is <u>propane</u> and kerosene. Propane for cooking and for heating will be a precious commodity. We heat with propane currently and the tank remains relatively sixty to seventy per-cent full. Also, we are accumulating small cans of propane for the <u>propane stove</u> in order to be able to cook. Propane and the proper size fittings are good to keep at all levels of preparedness but the need for this would probably start more at the <u>Robust </u>Pyramid level and continue through <u>Extreme</u> and <u>Off the Grid</u>.

We have purchased many <u>gas can containers </u>and we now store as much gasoline in them to hopefully run generators, vehicle, mini bike and all-terrain vehicle. We have two generators and store one in a Faraday Cage. This is not the case for everyone, but we have a beautiful twenty six gallon swimming pool which would very soon become a pestilent pool of nasty slime without the electricity to run the pool pump so we recently purchased a <u>120v emergency sump pump</u> which would be able to drain our pool via generator if necessary. A slow draining of the pool can also be done via siphoning with a garden hose as well. Ironic isn't it? So much water and we would be able to do nothing with it.

We have made sure to purchase <u>batteries</u> of all voltages but especially for <u>flashlights</u>. Making sure, of course, that we both know where each flashlight is in each room. We have also pur-chased rechargeable batteries and can use the solar power system as a recharger. It was a bit of an investment but we now own an <u>1800 watt solar power system</u> which can be used to directly run a chest freezer and small refrigerator indefinitely as well as some lights and some electronic equipment without using fuel. You can purchase one as a package for as little as about two thou-sand dollars. We have tested it and are keeping it also in a Faraday Cage. Should a true disaster occur, a solar system would also become incredibly valuable. Believe it or not, solar system packages are already "flying off the shelves". The thought of living without electricity for any extended length of time is mind blowing. So to us, these investments are truly worth it at least for some peace of mind.

Although is does not fit our décor in peace time so it has not been deployed, we have a <u>wood burning stove</u> with the correct piping and a window fitting all set to be put into action and given the downed trees in the forest that surrounds our property, we should be set for <u>firewood</u>. This is where having an <u>axe</u> handy comes into play. The idea of a freezing cold house due to lack of electricity for any length of time makes us shiver.

SELF DEFENSE
(Psychological)

Quite possibly, what may become even worse than the effects a disaster and the ensuing lack of electricity, food, water, heat, etc. on any level is what it will do to us psychologically. The magnitude of a man-made or natural catastrophe simply boggles the brain. We really cannot imagine or wrap our minds around just to what extent a disaster would bring us. Disaster is defined according to Merriam Webster.com as *"a sudden calamitous event bringing great damage, loss, or destruction"*. What would be our capacity to respond and react to a true disaster on an individual basis or a societal basis? As a species, our physiological and psychological reactions to a disaster are impossible for us to truly know. We do not want to speculate but we must. We must realize that our vulnerability is huge.

Will we be able to reframe and reorganize on a moment's notice? Our individual coping mechanisms will either help or hinder how we handle an emergency situation. Coping has been defined as *"constantly changing cognitive and behavioral efforts to manage specific external and internal demands that are appraised as taxing or exceeding the resources of the person"* (Lazarus & Folkman, Stress, Appraisal and Coping 1984, p. 141).

Our ability to focus on the given situation and our ability to confront and manage the situation, however stressful it may be, with a clear attitude of awareness of a plan and the regimented carrying out of that plan will be the difference between surviving and not surviving.

There is actually a hierarchy of phases of disaster which we find very interesting. According to the California Department of Mental Health as part of their Crisis Toolkit, they include the following:

Pre-Disaster Phase

Disasters vary in the amount of warning communities receive before they occur. For example, earthquakes typically hit with no warning; whereas, hurricanes and floods typically arrive within hours to days of warning. When there is no warning, survivors may feel more vulnerable, unsafe, and fearful of future unpredicted tragedies. The perception that they had no control over protecting themselves or their loved ones can be deeply distressing.

When people do not heed warnings and suffer losses as a result, they may experience guilt and self-blame. While they may have specific plans for how they might protect themselves in the future, they can be left with a sense of guilt or responsibility for what has occurred.

Impact Phase

The impact phase of a disaster can vary from the slow, low-threat buildup associated with some types of floods to the violent, dangerous, and destructive outcomes associated with tornadoes and explosions. The greater the scope, community destruction, and personal losses associated with the disaster, the greater the psychosocial effects.

Depending on the characteristics of the incident, people's reactions range from constricted, stunned, shock-like responses to the less common overt expressions of panic or hysteria. Most typically, people respond initially with confusion and disbelief, and focus on the survival and physical well-being of themselves and their loved ones. When families are in different geographic locations during the impact of a disaster (e.g., children at school, adults at work), survivors will experience considerable anxiety until they are reunited.

Heroic Phase

In the immediate aftermath of a disaster event, survival, rescuing others, and promoting safety are priorities. Evacuation to shelters, motels, or other homes may be necessary. For some, post-impact disorientation gives way to adrenaline-induced rescue behavior to save lives and protect property. While activity level may be high, actual productivity is often low. The capacity to assess risk may be impaired and injuries can result. Altruism is prominent among both survivors and emergency responders.

The conditions associated with evacuation and relocation have psychological significance. When there are physical hazards or family separations during the evacuation process, survivors often experience posttraumatic reactions. When the family unit is not together due to shelter requirements or other factors, an anxious focus on the welfare of those not present may detract from the attention necessary for immediate problem solving.

Honeymoon Phase

During the week to months following a disaster, formal governmental and volunteer assistance may be readily available. Community bonding occurs as a result of sharing the catastrophic experience and the giving and receiving of community support. Survivors may experience a short-lived sense of optimism that the help they will receive will make them whole again. When disaster mental health workers are visible and perceived as helpful during this phase, they are more readily accepted and have a foundation from which to provide assistance in the difficult phases ahead.

Disillusionment Phase

Over time, survivors go through an inventory process during which they begin to recognize the limits of available disaster assistance. They become physically exhausted due to enormous multiple demands, financial pressures, and the stress of relocation or living in a damaged home. The unrealistic optimism initially experienced can give way to discouragement and fatigue. As disaster assistance agencies and volunteer groups begin to pull out, survivors may feel abandoned and resentful. Survivors calculate the gap between the assistance they have received and what they will require to regain their former living conditions and lifestyle. Stressors abound—family discord, financial losses, bureaucratic hassles, time constraints, home reconstruction, relocation, and lack of recreation or leisure time. Health problems and exacerbations of pre-existing conditions emerge due to ongoing, unrelenting stress and fatigue. The larger community less impacted by the disaster has often returned to business as usual, which typically is discouraging and alienating for survivors. Ill will and resentment may surface in neighborhoods as survivors receive unequal monetary amounts for what they perceive to be equal or similar damage. Divisiveness and hostility among neighbors undermine community cohesion and support.

Reconstruction Phase

The reconstruction of physical property and recovery of emotional well-being may continue for years following the disaster. Survivors have realized that they will need to solve the problems of rebuilding their own homes, businesses, and lives largely by themselves and have gradually assumed the responsibility for doing so. With the construction of new residences, buildings, and roads comes another level of recognition of losses. Survivors are faced with the need to readjust to and integrate new surroundings as they continue to grieve losses. Emotional resources within the family may be exhausted, and social support from friends and family may be worn thin. When people come to see meaning, personal growth, and opportunity from their disaster experience despite their losses and pain, they are well on the road to recovery. While disasters may bring profound life-changing losses, they also bring the opportunity to recognize personal strengths and to reexamine life priorities. Individuals and communities progress through these phases at different rates, depending on the type of disaster and the degree and nature of disaster exposure. This progression may not be linear or sequential, as each person and community brings unique elements to the recovery process. Individual variables, such as psychological resilience, social support, and financial resources, influence a survivor's capacity to move through the phases. While there is always a risk of aligning expectations too rigidly with a developmental sequence, having an appreciation of the unfolding of psychosocial reactions to disaster is valuable.

U.S. Department of Health and Human Services, Substance Abuse and Mental Health Services Administration. (2000). Training manual for mental health and human services workers in major disasters, second edition. Washington, DC.

"Who would want to be the prey in a world full of hunters?" Alexia Purdy; Disarming

Faced with severe disorganization and serious lack, re-establishing ourselves on even a minimal level, let alone on a routine level will be extremely difficult. Our physical and mental needs will be highly distorted and the sense of being out of control might very well prevail, especially for those who have not prepared. As a society, the anxiousness, irritability, anger and panic will be to an extreme. Having said all of this, our reason for including this in the SELF DEFENSE section is plain to see.

SELF DEFENSE
(Physical)

Remember that thin veneer that we humans have and call "being civilized"? We, unfortunately, feel that for the majority, acting civilized in a disastrous event will not be the norm. So as part of our preparedness we have purchased weapons such as a 9mm hand gun and a shotgun and ammunition for them. We make sure to practice with them so we are well trained in caring for them and shooting well. As we write this book, ammunition is getting extremely scarce to procure also. We truly hope, however, that there will never be a need to use firearms or weapons for self-defense at any level of the Prepper Pyramid. And thankfully, where we live is far enough off the beaten path from major cities where we do not anticipate much need for protection, but we are prepared nonetheless. In the bigger cities, we imagine that severe civil unrest will occur. Here again, is a huge stress factor in having grown children who do live in big cities. We cannot even think about what might or could happen to them with respect to unrest in the form of rioting, shootings and thefts.

COMMUNICATION

Without a doubt, the inability to communicate during a crisis situation will be one of the most difficult for us to support. On a personal level, we cannot imagine the inability to communicate with our children to hear of their safety.

Effective communication on a country wide basis would help to ensure the maintaining of public awareness and safety and would help to get the correct equipment and support to where they are needed. According to the Federal Communication Commission, during an emergency, three main parts ensure emergency communications. The first is 911 call processing which is upheld by Public Safety Answering Points and call dispatching systems. The second is the Emergency Alert System and the third is radio/broadcast/cable TV station news. In the event of an emergency, the President of the United States decides when the Emergency Alert System will be sent nationally.

We know that the Federal Emergency Management Agency (FEMA) is responsible, in the case of a national disaster, to help prepare for an emergency at the state and local government level and on an individual level. We also know that Department of Homeland Security (DHS) is responsible for trying to prevent or reduce terrorism.

All well and good, so why are we not feeling warm and fuzzy about all that? Because should there be an EMP situation which would result in no electricity and no functioning vehicles to charge our cell phones, those of us with only cell phones are cut off. We would not be able to receive any news broadcasts on our televisions either. So as mentioned in Appendix F of this book, "short of smoke signals and mirrors", we really only have a couple of choices.

Since we are just the two of us here, walkie talkies will be put to good use should one of us venture into the forest to hunt or gather. These have a three hundred yard distance span. We currently do not own a Ham Radio or have a license but this is a future possibility. If you are a Ham radio operator or wish to become one, the Survival Communications books mentioned in Appendix F of this book can be extremely useful. Ham radios can use batteries and solar cells as a power source. Keeping a spare car battery is a plus. What we have done is purchase a Short-Wave radio to allow us to hear worldwide broadcasts and a wind-up am/fm radio. Both radios, along with batteries for the short wave radio and the walkie talkies, are in their own separate Faraday Cage.

LOCOMOTION

For some light reading we recommend the EMP Commission Critical National Infrastructures Report. http://empcommission.org/docs/A2473-EMP_Commission-7MB.pdf. Before we started our research into the Prepper world, we had no idea that an EMP could or would even exist, whatever the cause, let alone there being reports and commissions committed to studying its effects! The following is an excerpt from this EMP Commission Critical National Infrastructures Report, April 2008, p. 115-116 with regards to vehicles and trucks:

Automobiles

"The potential EMP vulnerability of automobiles derives from the use of built-in electronics that support multiple automotive functions. Electronic components were first introduced into automobiles in the late 1960s. As time passed and electronics technologies evolved, electronic applications in automobiles proliferated. Modern automobiles have as many as 100 microprocessors that control virtually all functions. While electronic applications have proliferated within automobiles, so too have application standards and electromagnetic interference and electromagnetic compatibility (EMI/EMC) practices.

Thus, while it might be expected that increased EMP vulnerability would accompany the proliferated electronics applications, this trend, at least in part, is mitigated by the increased application of EMI/EMC practices.

We tested a sample of 37 cars in an EMP simulation laboratory, with automobile vintages ranging from 1986 through 2002. Automobiles of these vintages include extensive electronics and represent a significant fraction of automobiles on the road today. The testing was conducted by exposing running and non-running automobiles to sequentially increasing EMP field intensities. If anomalous response (either temporary or permanent) was observed, the testing of that particular automobile was stopped. If no anomalous response was observed, the testing was continued up to the field intensity limits of the simulation capability (approximately 50 kV/m).

Automobiles were subjected to EMP environments under both engine turned off and engine turned on conditions. No effects were subsequently observed in those automobiles that were not turned on during EMP exposure. The most serious effect observed on running automobiles was that the motors in three cars stopped at field strengths of approximately 30 kV/m or above. In an actual EMP exposure, these vehicles would glide to a stop and require the driver to restart them. Electronics in the dashboard of one automobile were damaged and required repair. Other effects were relatively minor. Twenty-five automobiles exhibited malfunctions that could be considered only a nuisance (e.g., blinking dashboard lights) and did not require driver intervention to correct. Eight of the 37 cars tested did not exhibit any anomalous response.

Based on these test results, we expect few automobile effects at EMP field levels below 25 kV/m. Approximately 10 percent or more of the automobiles exposed to higher field levels may experience serious EMP effects, including engine stall, that require driver intervention to correct. We further expect that at least two out of three automobiles on the road will manifest some nuisance response at these higher field levels. The serious malfunctions could trigger car crashes on U.S. highways; the nuisance malfunctions could exacerbate this condition. The ultimate result of automobile EMP exposure could be triggered crashes that damage many more vehicles than are damaged by the EMP, the consequent loss of life, and multiple injuries."

Trucks

"As is the case for automobiles, the potential EMP vulnerability of trucks derives from the trend toward increasing use of electronics. We assessed the EMP vulnerability of trucks using an approach identical to that used for automobiles. Eighteen running and non-running trucks were exposed to simulated EMP in a laboratory. The intensity of the EMP fields was increased until either anomalous response was observed or simulator limits were reached. The trucks ranged from gasoline-powered pickup trucks to large diesel-powered tractors. Truck vintages ranged from 1991 to 2003.

Of the trucks that were not running during EMP exposure, none were subsequently affected during our test. Thirteen of the 18 trucks exhibited a response while running. Most seriously, three of the truck motors stopped. Two could be restarted immediately, but one required towing to a garage for repair. The other 10 trucks that responded exhibited relatively minor temporary responses that did not require driver intervention to correct.

Five of the 18 trucks tested did not exhibit any anomalous response up to field strengths of approximately 50 kV/m.

Based on these test results, we expect few truck effects at EMP field levels below approximately 12 kV/m. At higher field levels, 70 percent or more of the trucks on the road will manifest some anomalous response following EMP exposure. Approximately 15 percent or more of the trucks will experience engine stall, sometimes with permanent damage that the driver cannot correct.

Similar to the case for automobiles, the EMP impact on trucks could trigger vehicle crashes on U.S. highways. As a result, many more vehicles could be damaged than those damaged directly by EMP exposure."

Wow, Ok and … " In case of an EMP encounter…Research shows less than 10 percent of vehicles will stall when encountering an EMP, and most will start right back up again."
http://www.ehow.com/how_7928262_protect-car-emp.html.

Why is that very hard to believe? Whether by solar storm or nuclear detonation, even with all of the research and documentation, we do not know really to what extent our vehicles and trucks will be damaged. The tests that have been done have used a degree of electromagnetic pulse far less than could actually occur, we're sure. The only way to ensure no damage in an Off the Grid case is to have a metal garage or Faraday Cage large enough to have housed the vehicle.

The one thing, however, that is for sure is that while the electrical infrastructure would fail including all exposed generators, transportation, banking, food delivery and technology as we know it, we would not have fuel. Obtaining fuel after a disaster as such would become extremely difficult. The pumping of fuel would cease because there would be no fuel to pump! Gasoline pumps run on electricity, no electricity, no gas. In order to be somewhat prepared we have purchased gas can containers and keep them filled and rotate for auto gas to keep stored gas fresher longer. Although we have not purchased additives yet, we will. But, as opposed to perhaps having a non-running vehicle…we have heard of many who are trying to "EMP Proof" their vehicles such as the aforementioned metal garages. This is potentially NOT a good idea! What will you use the vehicle for? To go to the grocery store? The mall? The gas station? All of which probably will not be in operation. We all will have limited fuel even if we are storing backup in gasoline cans. We truly are better off saving the gasoline for intermittent use of a generator. Also, would you really want to be the driver of the ONLY vehicle driving through towns where many folks might be armed and desperate? A true dichotomy for sure.

Now on the upside of having a vehicle for use during a natural disaster is that one strategic approach is to use your vehicle to bring you to a "Bug Out" location. A loose definition of a "Bug Out Location" is a secluded place for you to go in the case of a disaster to be more safely away from the disaster and the possible civil unrest. So your vehicle now brings you to the Bug Out Location and becomes your Bug Out. You can take supplies with you, drive your vehicle to a safer place and wait. An example would be if you have land in a location that will not be affected by the disaster or the unrest. We keep physical and topographical maps on hand for such an event. We know this is not the norm, but it could very well be an option.

What we have done aside from some fuel savings is purchased a <u>mini bike</u>…(remember those)? We think this could be very effective in travel both within our own property and within the town/city should the need arise and to get to fishing holes! This too will have to be stored in a metal container until needed. Although we do not own an <u>All Terrain vehicle,</u> It would come in very handy in a country setting to aide in getting to hunting and fishing places. We have also made sure that our <u>bicycles</u> function, have air in the tires and are within reach for easy deployment.

TOILETRIES

The good people of the United States of America, for the most part, are obsessed with cleanliness. We have hundreds and even thousands of products to keep us clean, to make our hair shiny, to keep us from smelling from any part of our bodies, to brighten and whiten our teeth, to groom our finger and toe nails and keep us in sweet smelling clothes.

How do we do this? Sophisticated plumbing and glorious, hot, running water. Imagine a world harkened back to the early centuries of this country where stink and filth, stench and excrement were the norm. Could this once again happen in an Off the Grid situation? Quite honestly, not being able to bathe normally is unbelievable frightening for us. We will only make reference here to the items we have listed under the heading of TOILETRIES since there is no explanation really needed. We are trying, however, to gather as much of these items as possible and if we use them , we replace them as soon as possible. We're sure that there are more to add, but for now they are the basics.

EQUIPMENT AND MISCELLANEOUS

As far as these topics are concerned, we just make sure that we know where everything is housed and that we can get to them in a hurry if need be. The lists of EQUIPMENT AND MISCELLANEOUS could probably go on forever, but for starters we feel this is adequate.

"If we could see the miracle of a single flower clearly, our whole life would change" Prince
Gautama Siddhartha

As we are typing, we are looking out the side windows which face east in our home. The sun is shining, the sky is blue and there is a gentle breeze. What we are seeing is a picture perfect setting. Could it also be the perfect setting for a disaster, natural or man-made? Unfortunately, the answer is yes. But as prepared as we think we are and as aware as we think we are, the magnitude and the imminence we will not know until the time it occurs, if it occurs at all.

We, for now, even though we are Preppers, delight in the beauty of the blue sky, the sun, the breeze and the single flower. We are living a miracle, we are a miracle. We bow our heads in reverence for all that we have in this beautiful world and pray that it shall always remain so.

Prepping for Parents with Small Children

By

Alice Gunner

According to Merriam-Webster online*, the word *prepper* "…isn't in the dictionary."

When you search the word *prepper* in Wikipedia online**, you get redirected to the word *survivalism*, which is defined by Wiki as follows:

"Survivalism is a movement of individuals or groups (called survivalists or preppers) who are actively preparing for emergencies, including possible disruptions in social or political order, on scales from local to international. Survivalists often acquire emergency medical and self-defense training, stockpile food and water, prepare to become self-sufficient, and build structures (e.g., a survival retreat or an underground shelter) that may help them survive a catastrophe. Anticipated disruptions may include: Clusters of natural disasters, patterns of apocalyptic planetary crises, or "Earth Changes" (tornadoes, hurricanes, earthquakes, blizzards, solar storms, severe thunderstorms, floods, tsunamis). Anthropogenic disasters (chemical spills, release of radioactive materials, nuclear or conventional war, oppressive governments). The general collapse of society caused by the shortage or unavailability of resources such as electricity, fuel, food, or water. Financial disruption or economic collapse (caused by monetary manipulation, hyperinflation, deflation, or depression). A global pandemic. Widespread chaos or some other unexplained apocalyptic event."

And just for fun, I looked up the definition of the word *prepper* in the Urban Dictionary online*** and got a good laugh out of their definitions of the word, which are:

"1. **Prepper** – Someone who focuses on preparedness, generally for various worst-case scenarios like peak oil or Armageddon. Sometimes used to avoid the more loaded term *survivalist*. Some preppers focus on guns, others on sustainable agriculture.

2. **Prepper** – Someone who can't wait for the end of the world, and 'prepares' for it by hoarding food, guns, ammunition, water purification tablets, paracord, rice, MRE, camouflage clothing, Walmart gift cards, and pretend Tea Party 'money' that they think will be worth something someday. Often this fear/hope that society will end "any day now" is related to religious beliefs, distrust of a government they didn't vote for, and/or a shared delusion among their peers that only they are intelligent enough to "see the signs" of our collective impending doom. A strong paramilitary aspect usually goes with the Prepper lifestyle, even though most of them couldn't run a mile to save their own lives, never mind carrying some of the heaviest items possible on their backs; batteries, water, bullets, and gold. Up to this point 100% of "preppers" have been wrong so far, a trend likely to continue for a very long time. It has been theorized that in the unlikely event of an actual catastrophe large enough to actually destroy society, that Preppers would be the first to be 'pushed out' by a new society, since honestly, who wants a bunch of ignorant aggressive selfish loudmouth jerkoffs around when it's time for everyone to put aside their differences and rebuild a new society?

Steve: "Did you see that guy buying all those shovels and batteries? What's up with that?"

Jay: "Yeah… he's a Prepper. He thinks he will be the only one to survive whatever race war or zombie attack his church or Alex Jones predicted.""

Comical? Yes, to me anyway. Offensive? Maybe, to some. I still felt it worthy to share for, at minimum, those with a good sense of humor.

When my husband and I were approached about contributing to this book from the prepper perspective of 'a married couple with young children', we felt largely unworthy. Sure, we are a married couple with young children and, sure, we have "prepped" to a certain degree, but we are far from being as prepared as some self-proclaimed preppers, survivalists and homesteaders. If you've ever seen the show *Doomsday Preppers*, I can assure you we are nowhere near as prepared as most folks on that show are. But after discussing it further, we felt like maybe we would have something to offer others that are interested in "prepping" without 'going off the deep end' like many feel some folks do. There really can be a balance of prepping for your family without getting the crazy looks from people within your circle of friends because "now *you* jumped on the bandwagon, too". To that extent, we feel honored to share our experiences and plans with you coming from an average, middle-class American family.

So, why do we prep to begin with? That seems to be a loaded question. Our knee-jerk response is the old adage "It's better to be safe than sorry!". As every parent knows, the second you bring a child in to this world you very quickly realize that you are no longer only responsible for yourself. You instantly become responsible for this tiny little person, like an extension of yourself. *No pressure or anything, but here's your brand new baby. You will be responsible for maintaining his/her optimal physical, mental, emotional and spiritual health for the next 18 years, at a bare minimum. Oh, and by the way, you'll also have to feed, clothe, protect, nurture, entertain, teach and love this little person, too.* That's a whole lot of pressure and responsibility, but most parents know that it's more than worth it to raise a family. We have 3 *'littles'* in our family that we're graciously responsible for. There's not much in this life that we fear, but the fear of failing any one of them at any point in their lives is heart wrenching for us to ponder. And, so, this is another major reason why we prep; however, realistically, to fully understand why we do what we do, I'll have to go back in time to explain how I feel prepping is innately ingrained within me.

My husband and I are from the late 70's/early 80's generation. We were both raised in the same large, metropolitan city. We grew up riding our bikes with our friends until the street lights came on, playing Pac Man, Tetris and Super Mario Bros., making mixed tapes of our favorite radio songs and drinking from the garden hose like most suburban kids of our time. Life was good. We had microwaves and remote controls for our TV's and even got pagers once our parents felt we were old enough. Okay, who am I kidding? Once we drove our parents crazy enough with our incessant requests for something that "all our friends had" and we desperately needed, as well. We relished in the advancements of technology that we continuously got to reap the benefits from. I'd even venture to say that our generation was the first to watch technology advancements explode and start getting better and better, faster and faster. And although this was an exciting and promising time to grow up in, most of our generation lacked the knowledge of what life was like before all these advancements in technology. What life was like for our parents, who were raised on farms milking cows, having to share neighborhood telephone lines, family time being piled around a radio to listen to their favorite radio show, instead of watching a TV. I feel extremely lucky that I got to grow up knowing what life would be like without all the fascinating technology that was so quickly taking over. I had the privilege of learning and participating in things that sounded like ancient history to most of my friends, and here's why...

I was born the eldest of two to a "Mountain Man" trucker and a self-proclaimed Tom-boy businesswoman. My parents loved to be outdoors. They were avid hunters, fishermen, and camping extraordinaires. My younger sister and I got to grow up learning a lot of things about what life was really like 'back in the olden days' because of our nature-loving parents.

We had a cabin up north that we frequented on a regular basis. This cabin was literally built from the ground up by my mom's mother and father, with the help of her and her two brothers. What a fantastic adventure this cabin was! Well, my mom and her brothers never looked at it that way when they were teenagers being forced to drive up north to go work on the cabin again instead of hanging out with their friends on the weekends. But what a great adventure and experience for my sister and I to grow up with! Our cabin had no running electricity (although many moons down the road, my grandpa did finally succumb to hard wiring in real electricity), so when we arrived there each time, the first thing we'd have to do upon entering was light a lantern. Like a real, kerosene lantern that always gave a good '*whoosh*' once it was lit. After lighting the lantern, we'd go down beneath the porch and pull out that old, clunky generator. After a few good pulls, my dad usually had it purring like a (loud) kitty. Okay, now we *did* have electricity for some things, mainly lights and the old refrigerators that were kept there. Now it was time to get the place warm. We'd go get some pre-cut timber (which was hand cut with an axe and a wedge from previous visits) from under an old tarp and start loading up the wood stove. My sister and I did learn how to build a pretty mean fire, if I do say so myself! Once the wood stove was burning good, we could finally start unpacking. Inevitably, someone *had* to pee. Although there was a legitimate, full-fledged outhouse just a hop, skip and a jump away from the cabin (which *was* the ONLY bathroom option short of squatting in the woods while my mom and her brothers grew up building the cabin), thankfully there were *real* toilets by the time my sister and I got to enjoy the cabin (Hey, you can take the girl outta the city, but you can't take the city outta the girl!)! The only catch was running water to flush said toilets… Ahh, running water? Nope, no such thing at the cabin. You see, the cabin had a gutter system that drained in to rain barrels that then drained in to a giant cistern underneath the cabin, and that's where our water came from. I vividly remember pulling up that large piece of plywood from the kitchen floor, pulling up the next big wooden lid and looking down in to the abyss we called our water storage, aka the cistern. We would pour Clorox bleach down in it almost every time we visited. Clearly, this was not the water we drank, but it was the water we flushed toilets with, washed our hair and bodies with and washed all our dishes with (after boiling some of it). But how did we get the water out of that giant abyss of a cistern? Well, we had a cast iron hand pump attached to the counter at the sink in the kitchen that was piped down to the cistern. We would always have to use our own water to prime the pump in order to get it flowing, but once it was primed, that water was flowing like Niagara Falls. We filled giant, metal trash cans with the water and used buckets to dip out any water we needed. An underground septic tank is what collected all this water any time it went down the drain, but we were taught about conservation to limit unnecessary waste. You know, 'If it's yellow, let it mellow. If it's brown, flush it down'. This same conservation mentality was carried over in to our normal lives at home for as far back as I can remember. If you're not in a room anymore, turn the lights off. If you had two paper plates and the bottom one was still clean by the time you were done, you saved it. If you washed your hands at the kitchen sink and used a paper towel to dry your hands, that damp paper towel was saved on the counter and undoubtedly could be used a second time for something at some point. And of course there was always the *'Were you raised in a barn?!? CLOSE THE DOOR!!'* .

So, you may be wondering what all this has to do with prepping? Well, simply put, my parents were always prepared. Being prepared was not something they did out of fear of any one thing in particular happening, but rather out of the enlightenment and relief they felt knowing that they were at least prepared *if* something actually did happen. We always came to the cabin with more food, water and supplies then we could ever possibly need, but it didn't matter, because that's just what they did. Same old adage…It's better to be safe than sorry. In addition to being prepared, I feel that these life experiences I learned about and participated in could very likely serve me well someday if something ever did cause us to have to revert back to an 'old fashioned' way of doing things. It's very easy to take our fast-paced, technology-filled lives for granted. At least I seek comfort in knowing that I have some knowledge of how to survive without all the luxuries most American's enjoy on a daily basis.

At home, we had a giant walk-in pantry that had shelves from the floor all the way to the ceiling. That pantry was always full of food. I remember seeing all kinds of shiny, unmarked No. 10 cans that were full of things like potato pearls and dried apples. I rarely remember ever actually eating any of them, but my mom was notorious for being sneaky when it came to food (Case and point: I learned later in my adult life that the Aunt Jemima syrup I grew up eating was really Log Cabin syrup transferred in to that Aunt Jemima bottle over and over again, because "you didn't like any kind of syrup except good 'ol Aunt Jemima".). We also had MRE's loaded up on those shelves. I swear there was enough food in that pantry to feed an army. I never really chalked this food overload up to anything more than my mom and her "pack rat" tendencies. But, I did always know that it was there, it seemingly lasted an eternity and we'd never go hungry. We also always had a good supply of 5 gallon Crystal water bottles that we used with a water dispenser for our drinking water. And then there were the guns and ammo. I'm pretty sure my dad kept enough guns and ammo to make it through WW3. Again, I always chalked this up to the fact that my parents loved to shoot and hunt, therefore finding it necessary to have more than you know what to do with so you'll never run out.

All these things from my childhood are why I feel like prepping has been innately ingrained in to my being. I never realized it at the time, but I was "conditioned" to always keep more than I need in case I do need it someday and conserve what I do have for the same reasons. I do believe that the experiences I lived while growing up really did shape my understanding of why one should stay prepared.

Now, fast forward back to more recent years. After my husband and I got married, we decided we wanted out of the rat race of the big metropolitan city we were raised in. Although we both had great childhoods in this city, we both longed to raise our family in a slower pace of life, bringing back some of the basics like growing our own garden, raising chickens and enjoying nature. You can't really enjoy everything nature has to offer when you live in a cookie-cutter home with 8ft block fenced in back yards, or at least that's how we felt. So, we loaded our oldest child and all our belongings up and happily transplanted our roots in a gorgeous rural setting in the South at the foothills of the Appalachian Mountains, surrounded by stunning green foliage and water sources everywhere you look. We were lucky enough to find our perfect home sitting on just over 5 acres of beauty, complete with a creek and brilliant pasture views. It was such a breath of fresh air (both literally and figuratively) to no longer be surrounded by concrete, pollution and rush hour traffic. Moving to this picturesque new setting afforded us the ability to make a large plot for our very own vegetable garden, build a rather large coop for those chickens we wanted to raise and a nice gun range where we could freely enjoy using all the guns we own and both were raised shooting.

We felt like this new lifestyle was going to give our children the life I felt like I was living every time I was up at our cabin, minus the lack of common commodities like instant electricity and running water. Who knows? Maybe by the time they grow up and are ready to spread their wings, they'll be so tired of living in a sleepy little town that they'll fly away to a big city to raise their families. We truly hope not, but let's face it, that's exactly what we did to our parents in reverse order.

So, it's come the time to share our perspective on prepping as a family with young children. In a world surrounded by religious and political wars, the declining value of a dollar and inflation, pollution and a depleting ozone layer, processed and convenience foods, GMO's, BPA, government cover-ups, corrupt corporations, Big Pharma and convoluted mainstream media just to name a few, we feel like there's a gazillion reasons why we should stay prepared. My husband and I are very optimistic people. We do believe in *good* things, *good* people and *good* thoughts to help us live a *good* life. We are not preppers out of fear of any one thing happening to us, but rather out of preparedness in the event that anything *could* happen that would require us to depend on ourselves for our own survival, and not our government. Simply put, we want to be prepared to keep our family as healthy and comfortable as possible if any one of a gazillion different "what ifs" were to happen.

I believe that the two biggest challenges to prepping are the extra cost of additional food/supplies and having the storage space to store any additional food/supplies. I've learned in my prepping journey that if you make a plan as to what you want to have prepared, you can slowly pick up these additional items a little bit at a time, here and there so as to not hit the pocketbook so hard. That's how we've been adding to our supply. It helps to ease the anxiety over the cost of stocking additional items that you know you don't necessarily need right now. Having adequate storage space is important, too. I understand that many families that would like to prep simply do not have adequate space to store any items they're able to obtain. This is where I've gotten a little bit creative. Think about any and all unused spaces within your home: under beds, in closets and maybe even a garage. Luckily for us, we do have a good bit of space that can be utilized to store things, but we could always use more. As I'm writing this, we have 1 gallon bottles of water lined up under one of our children's beds. It's no skin off our backs to store it there and, if nothing else, it prevents our '*little*' from kicking his toys under his bed when it's time to clean his room. We just try to use the space we do have to its greatest potential.

Our prepping journey is an ongoing process. We've acknowledged the fact that we do want to be as prepared as we possibly can be, but to be 100% prepared for any one type of catastrophe is no easy feat. There are many things we still want to obtain and do to work towards being self-reliant and self-sustaining, but these things cannot happen all at once. So, with that said, we take comfort in knowing that what we have prepared up to this point would at least be enough to get us through any short-term situation that required us to utilize our prepared items. As for the rest of the things we'd like to do and have, we remain optimistic about reaching our goals without feeling overwhelmed or burdened by when and how we will complete those preparation goals.

The Prepper Pyramid, as described in this book, is a 5 step pyramid to identify 5 different timeframe situations of preparedness, which are:

Minimal Preparedness= A few days
Basic Preparedness= Up to a month
Robust Preparedness= 1-3 months
Extreme Preparedness= 3-12 months
Off-The-Grid Preparedness= More than a year

Each level builds upon the level beneath it. In other words, at the bottom of the pyramid is the "Minimal Preparedness" items and each level above this would require the items at the lowest levels, as well as more. I will go through each level in the Prepper Pyramid to share our perspective and personal preparedness for each level.

MINIMAL PREPAREDNESS (a few days)

I'm going to go out on a limb and presume that most *normal* (and I use that term *VERY* lightly) American families keep enough food and supplies in their home to make it through a few days. Every home in America has lost power for a few hours at some point or another, whether it be from weather or otherwise. So I'm assuming most know where their flashlights and candles are and have enough food in their cabinets and fridge to keep everyone content for a few days, if need be. If you're reading this and you don't at least have enough to survive a few days without power, please, please at a bare minimum prepare for this. I believe everyone should be prepared for surviving a few days when things like storms and rolling blackouts can all too commonly cut us off from our electricity-filled lives.

Our very first winter in our new home here in the South was an interesting one. Our area experienced one of the worst ice storms this region had seen in a long time, and we were without power for a solid 3 days and could not venture out for supplies of any kind. Had we been able to run up to the store for supplies, I assure you there would've been no milk or bread, because for some reason, that's what Southerner's load up on anytime there's a threat of imminent weather. Aside from needing food and water, having a heat source to keep us warm in the dead of winter surrounded by layers of ice was a must! Lucky for us, our home has two propane fireplaces that require no electricity to function. If it wasn't for those fireplaces and the propane that was in our tank, we'd have been a lot worse off than we were. Maybe not necessarily worse off, but definitely much less comfortable. It was an interesting time for us to see what life would be like without the everyday commodities of electricity and (although we had running water, our water heater required electricity to run) hot water. Its times like these that you realize how grateful you are for the little luxuries we have in this life. We used our propane grill to cook food and only got in to our fridge and freezer with calculated intent. We had every flashlight we owned and candles strategically placed for ample, but safe, light. At the time of this event, we still only had our first *'little'* that we were responsible for. Keeping him entertained was a challenge, because how do you keep a TV loving, video game junky child busy for 3 days straight with no power!?! We managed to make it work. We colored and drew pictures, sang songs and danced around, read stories and even bundled up to play outside. By the 2nd day in to our "adventure" many of our friends that lived in neighborhoods had already had their power restored. (Side note- This event made us realize that when it comes to who gets their power restored first, the power company cares more about the neighborhoods and communities first and us rural folks last.) Thankfully, we had some friends that graciously loaned us their generator once their power was restored so we could at least provide power to our refrigerator (before we lost all the food in it) and our hot water heater (so we could take a much desired hot shower). That was a huge blessing and made us think very long and hard about buying ourselves our very own generator after the whole fiasco ended. And then we got back to our normal day to day and that desire slowly went by the wayside for the time being (I'll touch on this again in later pyramid steps). So, long story short, we survived our first ice storm! And in all reality, as inconvenient as it was, it wasn't too awful and it was an experience that helped shape our desire to be prepared for these kinds of events, especially not knowing if this was "the norm" for living out here.

I've prepared a list of what I believe to be the essential items needed to survive a "Minimal" situation:

Food – What you have in your cabinets or pantry is probably sufficient, but if it's not, then at least have enough canned goods (soup, chili, vegetables, stew, etc.) and jarred goods (pasta sauce) to feed your family for a few days, at a bare minimum. Don't forget a good can opener or two, as well… This will make a world of difference when it comes to effectively getting in to those canned goods.

Water – If you have running water, then you're in good shape, but it's always a good idea to keep a case of bottled water stored for "just in case". Water is needed not only to drink, but to cook with and, if necessary, clean with (washing hands/faces, dishes, etc.).

Heat source (for colder months) – Keep sufficient blankets to keep warm. If you have another heat source in your home, such as a fireplace or wood stove (traditional or gas), be sure to have plenty of kindling, wood, matches or propane/natural gas to utilize this important asset. If you don't have any heat source other than blankets, you could look in to possibly purchasing some kind of non-electric heat alternative, such as a propane or kerosene space heater. These types of heaters range in price from $80-$350, respectively. (Side note- These types of heaters can be dangerous, so always follow the manufacturer's manual on use and safety!) We always keep a few 5 gallon propane tanks filled and at least 5 gallons of gasoline at all times.

Light source – Flashlights are the easiest and cheapest to keep around your house, but having sufficient batteries to power your flashlights are a must, too! You can also use candles (make sure you have matches and/or lighters to light), lanterns (both traditional and battery-powered) and even glow sticks.

Cooking source – This may be a luxury to some, but it certainly makes a world of difference when it comes down to eating cold soup out of a can or warm soup out of a bowl. Alternative cooking sources include barbeque grills (both charcoal and gas), camping stoves (generally gas powered) or even a Dutch oven used in an outdoor fire pit. Due to carbon monoxide risks, never use any of these cooking sources inside your home!

Toiletries – You're still going to need toilet paper and your toothbrush and toothpaste, even if the power is out. Chances are you may not get to shower for a few days, but having soap is still important to keep yourself and family clean. Any other feminine products would be important to have on hand, as well.

Entertainment – If you have kids, they're going to need entertainment! This is when keeping things like water color paints, crayons and markers on hand comes in very handy. Books and puzzles are a good resource to keep *'littles'* busy, as well. Let your imagination run wild, because this may very well end up being the most frustrating part of being without power and/or other luxuries that kids these days are used to having at their fingertips. You'll have to let your creativity flow when it comes to this one!

Communication – Unless you live under a rock or just refuse to join the rest of the majority, someone in your family undoubtedly owns a cell phone. As long as it's charged and you use it sparingly so as to not waste what battery life is left, this could be a very valuable item to have during any kind of situation. Communication is always essential for any situation, if for nothing else but use in emergencies. CB radios could also be used during such an event, but most people don't keep CB radios lying around the house these days. There are a lot of HAM radio operators from one end of the country to the other, so knowing where the closest ones to you are could prove very valuable. You can easily get a list of all the registered HAM operators in your area by obtaining the book Survival Communications by author and licensed HAM operator, John Parnell. A NOAA Weather Alert Radio is also a very good item to have. We have one in our home that obnoxiously goes off every Wednesday as the National Weather Service runs its weekly tests. As annoying as it can be at times, it's such an important asset to have, because it keeps us up to date on any dangerous weather scenarios in our immediate area and it's backed up with batteries, so it will still function during a power outage. Get the kind of radio that receives both NOAA and your local radio stations. NOAA is great for the big picture, but you also need to be aware of your local area. Make sure that the radio can operate off batteries. These types of radios are reasonably priced as low as $30, which is what I believe we paid for ours.

BASIC PREPAREDNESS (up to a month)

This is where being a wholesale club member comes in handy. My husband and I are members of such a "club"; you know the ones I'm talking about…Sam's Club, Costco, etc. We truly believe buying in bulk saves us a good bit of money. I'd be lying if I said it's easy to budget these trips to this said wholesale club, because, let's face it, if I can get in and out of there for under $250 I'm doing good. We have been able to find a system that works for us, without breaking the bank. The benefit is that we really do end up saving a lot of money in the long run by shopping there, and we rarely run out of our most commonly used items. There are only certain things that I notoriously buy when I go on these shopping trips, which usually equate to about once a month in frequency. These are the things I tend to buy most while on these shopping trips: toilet paper, paper towels, dog food, cleaning supplies (like disinfecting wipes and liquid dish soap), laundry detergent, Clorox bleach, bar soap, wipes (although our *'littles'* are no longer babies, every one still likes a clean bum), trash bags, beer and alcohol (for Mommy & Daddy's sippy cups), and food products like chicken breasts, hamburger meat, coffee, shredded cheese, canned goods and some frozen, "quick meal" products. Clearly, if you're going to buy in bulk, you need to have the space to store everything. This gets challenging at times, but it's so worth it to not have those *'OMG, we only have 1 roll of toilet paper left and don't get paid for another week!'* moments. Very rarely do I ever run out of these items, but only because I constantly stay on top of what we have and what we need. We do have an extra refrigerator and upright freezer in our basement to keep our cold/frozen food items in. I know this may not be an option for some, but we're gracious that we have the space to have these additional appliances in our home.

Another key to having things in bulk is to always rotate out the old to the front and the new to the back. For example, when I get home with a new case of green beans and corn, I pull all my green beans and corn in my cabinet out so I can put the new ones in back, thus making sure the older cans get eaten before the newer cans do. I do this with everything, even non-food products, and it's helpful to know that I never really need to worry about something being close to its expiration date. (Side note- Be sure to reference Appendix A and Appendix B in this book for food storage guidelines and shelf life!)

Something else I do to avoid the *'Oh no, we're out of (blank) again!'* scenarios, is that I always keep an *'extra'* of our most commonly used items in my food pantry. For example, I always have an extra ketchup, jelly, peanut butter, salad dressing, salsa and cooking oil (just to name a few) in stock in my cabinet. When what's in the fridge gets used and the *'extra'* from the cabinet gets brought out and opened, I immediately put that item on my shopping list so I can replace my backup once again. Although it's not rocket science, this process works for us and helps us to always have more than we need.

Because of my shopping habits, I feel that what I generally keep in my food pantry, refrigerators and freezers would be enough to keep my family fed for up to a month on a "Basic" level. Sure, I'd have to stretch what we have a little further than normal and get very creative on putting meals together, but I do feel that what we keep on hand on a regular basis would last up to a month, if necessary. Obviously, we'd have to plan on using refrigerated and frozen items first to keep from losing valuable food, but we could make it work with what we have.

Building upon the list I provided in the "Minimal" preparedness section (food, water, heat source, light source, cooking source, toiletries, entertainment, and communication), there are obviously more items you would need to survive a catastrophic situation for up to a month, instead of just a few days. I've recently read of 'The Rule of 3' which basically states that a human can go three minutes without air, three hours without heat, three days without water and three weeks without food. I can't vouch for the accuracy of this 'rule', but it does sound about right to me. If nothing else, it seems like a good rule of thumb to keep in the good 'ol memory bank upstairs.

Food – When prepping on a "Basic" level, one must calculate how much food their family would need per day to feed them for up to a month. Choosing to store items with long shelf lives would be ideal for a situation like this. Canned goods, jarred goods and dry foods, such as pastas and rice, are good to stock up on since they do tend to have a long shelf life. Refer to Appendix A for actual food storage guidelines, but it's my personal opinion that a majority of foods (especially canned goods and dry foods) are still good and edible for much longer than what their expiration date reads. Generally speaking, it's always been my understanding that as long as a canned good is not swollen or dented, whatever is inside is likely still safe to eat even if it is past its expiration date. Obviously, this notion would be on a case by case basis and certainly needs to be taken with a grain of salt. I'm certainly not an expert on the subject, so I would encourage all to use their common sense when it comes to feeding your family something that may or may not be expired.

Water – We all know water is essential for life. Our bodies can't go more than a few days without it. It has been said that it is necessary to have 1 gallon of water per person, per day for survival. I'm not sure who came up with this figure, but when you factor in what you need to drink, cook with and keep clean with, it does sound logical. We are a family of 5, which means we would need to store approximately 150 gallons of water to survive a month. That's an awful lot of water to store! An average 24 bottle case of water yields just over 3 gallons of water total, so a 3-day supply of water for our family would mean that we need at least 5 cases of bottled water. Water purification tablets are a great idea to keep stocked up on. This way, in a desperate situation, you could likely drink water from other sources, such as a stream, lake, or even rain water (if you collect it) by purifying it to at least make it potable. You can find decent prices on water purification tablets on the internet from a lot of different popular websites, like Amazon. Another noteworthy product to mention is a "waterBOB®" (this is the particular brand name, but there are other similar products that go by different names), which is for emergency drinking water storage. It's a great concept if we got any kind of notice that a catastrophe was coming. It is a food-grade plastic bladder that fits in to your bathtub. You just put the sleeve up over your bathtub faucet and let it fill to capacity. It only takes about 20 minutes to fill, stores up to 100 gallons of tap water, comes with a pump to dispense the water and keeps your water safe to consume for up to 4 weeks. They are relatively cheap averaging around $30. We have not purchased one yet, but intend to definitely add one or two to our prepping arsenal.

Medicine – If anyone in your household takes prescription medicine, it's important to stay on top of your refills to have as much as possible in a crisis situation. Another important thing to consider is multi-vitamins. If you have a good stock of multi-vitamins for both adults and children, this could help ease the angst of feeling like your family is not being fed enough nutrition. It's certainly no substitution for real food, but it could make a world of difference in the realm of health and nutrition. I always have your basic over-the-counter medications on hand, too. I keep the most important ones like pain relievers, antacids, allergy meds, etc. Another thing I do is keep any prescription medications that do not get finished. I know this is not recommended, but if I have a few antibiotic pills or pain medication left over from something, I will always keep it for the off chance that it may be needed by someone else in my family for something else someday. I would never give anyone in my family old medication in a normal situation environment, but I keep them on hand so I do have some options if going to the doctor or ER is not an option due to some kind of crisis situation.

First Aid Kit – I failed to mention this under my "Minimal" perspective, but having a good First Aid Kit readily available is extremely important. Something as simple as a cut or scrape could easily turn in to an infection if not properly cleaned and taken care of. We've acquired many

First Aid Kits over the years, and I've combined all of them in to one large First Aid Kit that has just about everything from bandages to antiseptic to tweezers in it.

ROBUST PREPAREDNESS (1-3 months)

If we ever reach this level of the Prepper Pyramid, something's gone majorly wrong. Regardless of what the crisis or emergency situation is, if I have to independently fend for my family and myself for more than a month, then this would generally indicate that something terrible has happened and we better start acknowledging the need for possible "Extreme or Off-the-Grid" survival. For my husband and I, this level in the Prepper Pyramid is where our true and calculated *prepping* begins.

So, we've already established that we are prepared on a "Minimal" and "Basic" level just by how we shop and store food and commonly used supplies in our home. Our "Robust" prepping takes on a whole new level. This is where knowing how to plant and maintain a garden comes in. It's also where having egg laying hens' turns from sharing our plentiful farm-fresh eggs with our friends and neighbors in to using eggs to feed our family on an almost regular basis. It changes from being a hobby to a necessity. So, staying on top of having enough chicken feed is vital, although we could always let them out to graze as yard chickens if and when we run out of chicken feed. The good news is that you can feed chickens almost anything humans eat, and although I doubt we'd be wasting much of anything during a time like this, we could feed them food scraps if necessary. The great thing about chicken eggs is that they have a ton of nutritional value. I've even heard that an egg has everything the human body needs to survive, thus suggesting that a human could survive off eating eggs alone; however, I've never truly found any documentation to validate this claim.

My younger sister has been on her own prepping journey for herself and her family for some time now. I must admit that she has done a lot of research on her own and shared a lot of her knowledge with me when it comes to becoming a self-sustaining survivalist. With that said, it was she who found our best option for purchasing dried foods with extended shelf lives. Remember those shiny No. 10 cans full of dried potato pearls and apples that I mentioned having as a child in the beginning of this writing? Well, she found an LDS (aka Mormon) canning facility in our state that sells their quality products to the public, in addition to their members. Through her intense research, she established that this would be our best option as far as quality and cost is concerned. The two of us went down there and stocked up on what we could. Everything we purchased came in sealed No. 10 cans, complete with an oxygen absorber inside and a product/nutritional label on the outside. All of these cans have a sealed 30 year shelf life if kept in a dry storage space at or below 75 degrees Fahrenheit. Once the cans are opened, they have a 2 year shelf life if stored in the same conditions. I spent less than $200, and this is everything I purchased:

> (3) cans of dehydrated apple slices, 16 servings per can
>
> (4) cans of dried pinto beans, 50 servings per can
>
> (1) can of dried white beans, 49 servings per can
>
> (4) cans of potato flakes, 39 servings per can

(3) cans of white rice, 57 servings per can

(7) cans of quick oats, 27 servings per can

(3) cans of nonfat dry milk, 69 servings per can

(1) can of dehydrated chopped onion, 318 servings per can

(1) can each of enriched wheat flour, hard red wheat and hard white wheat, which would be used to make dough and breads, etc.

(1) 20lb box of elbow macaroni

(1) 52lb bag of sugar

The last two items I listed must be packaged by me. I will put the elbow macaroni and the sugar each in a 5 gallon food-grade bucket with an oxygen absorber to extend their shelf lives to be closer to those in the No. 10 cans. In addition to the items that I purchased at the LDS canning facility, I've also added a few more things to our stash. I've purchased a 4lb box of salt, a 1lb container of black pepper and a 1lb container of garlic powder. The idea behind the sugar, salt, pepper, garlic powder and dehydrated chopped onion is that if we had to resort to using this food, at least I'd have some things to "spice" up whatever I'm able to make in hopes that these new foods would be more palatable. They're certainly not necessary for adequate nutrition, but they would certainly make whatever nutrition I serve more desirable. Anyone who has children knows this is important, especially in the case of picky eaters.

I'd be lying to you if I told you how long I anticipate the items I've purchased will actually last my family. We do feel like it's a good start, though. The one thing that the LDS canning facility did not offer is any kind of dehydrated meats. I would like to stock up on several cans of dehydrated meats, but I'm still in the process of trying to sort through my options to find the best quality products at the best prices.

Another option many homesteaders choose is to can their own food using jars. It's an age old practice and rather easy to do, from what I've learned. We've thought about canning our own vegetables and such, but haven't ever quite moved past talking about it. It's a great alternative to buying canned dry foods like we've done. It's always an option we may choose to start doing at any time.

Aside from food and water storage, we've also stocked additional non-food items, such as Clorox bleach, toilet paper and paper towels on the "Robust" level of the pyramid.

EXTREME PREPAREDNESS (3-12 months) and OFF-THE-GRID PREPAREDNESS (>1 year)

You'll notice that I've paired the last two levels of the Prepper Pyramid together. I did this, because I really can't see much of a difference from one level to the other. If we ever got to this point regardless of cause, it probably means there is or will soon be a total and complete economic collapse of all government and financial systems. Let's face it, if we're all left to fend for ourselves from a crisis or emergency situation for more than 3 months, then we more than likely will be put in a position of 'fight or flight' for survival. If we make it to either of these levels, chances are we will have no choice but to expect life to revert back to a much earlier place and time; back to more of a simple, Amish way of living; back to a time before we had any real form of technology or modern-day luxury. Those that survive such a hardship would likely have to learn a life of living off the land and self-sustained survival. The banks wouldn't be coming to take our homes away, the credit card companies wouldn't be tracking us down for our late bills and the government would certainly not be knocking on our doors to offer us any kind of help or support. Instead, we'd end up having to pull together to survive; families, friends and neighbors would have to join forces to share food, water, resources and knowledge. I see this type of situation as the end of the world as we know it. It would be the end of what we know and the beginning of what our new life would look like. I'm not trying to be 'Debbie Downer' here, but I don't see any other realistic way to look at such a dire situation. Survival of the fittest and most prepared would be the only people likely to survive such a situation.

My husband and I have discussed this level of preparedness on many occasions. We've tossed ideas around on what we'd do and how we'd do it. Ultimately, already living a life off the grid from power and water companies would make this situation a little easier to swallow if it ever did happen. Our dependence of power from power companies, water from water companies and food from grocery stores almost makes us slaves to them. We can't live without them, unless we move our homes and families off the grid before a crisis situation ever takes place. This is a very expensive and lengthy process and seems almost impossible in today's day and age. My husband and I recently bought in to the Power 4 Patriots system, which claims that through manuals and DVDs, they will teach you how to build solar panels and remove your home off the power grid for good. It is supposed to be explained in easy to understand, Layman's terms with reasonable costs on supplies from your local home improvement store(s). This is their claim:

"*Power4Patriots*, the simple, step-by-step system that can help you pull the plug on the power monopolies and be more self-reliant."**** Although we haven't actually dove in to the manuals and DVDs yet, we do intend on doing so at some point soon to see if it really will be as easy as they claim to get "off the grid". I don't know anyone that wouldn't love to stop paying for electricity!

Regardless of whether or not we do end up going all solar to get off the grid, we're still toying with the idea of buying a generator. It is really a sensible thing to have, but we're still trying to weigh our options and justify the cost. Another think we've talked about doing is replacing our propane fireplaces with real wood burning fireplaces. It would be easier for us to find and use wood then it would be to replenish an empty propane tank during a long crisis situation. A real fireplace would not only be a good source of heat, but could also be used as a cooking source, as well.

We've discussed how this level of preparedness would require us to live off our own land, which thankfully we have. We'd need heirloom seeds to grow a fruit and vegetable garden. Starting a compost pile would be a fantastic way to reduce our waste and have a great fertilizer to help grow our garden. We'd also need guns and ammunition to hunt our land for food. We've even bounced the idea of burying a large storage container underground in our backyard. We could use it as a hidden storage for our food, water, supplies and guns/ammo. We could even use it as a shelter for our family, if needed. We only recently learned of what a Faraday cage/box is. Although we understand its concept, we haven't put much thought in to making or getting one just yet. It's definitely not a bad idea, though. If we get one, we'd probably keep, at minimum, a few flashlights, some two-way radios and a weather radio inside.

Living in the rural setting we do is the most ideal place to be in the event of any catastrophic event that forced us in to these last levels of the Prepper Pyramid. There would be widespread panic and pandemonium that would start in large cities and spread outward from there. People would likely lose all sense of integrity, morals and values if it meant keeping their family alive. People would possibly use firearms to steal food, water and supplies from others they know have prepared for such a circumstance. We would certainly use firearms to protect our family, our home and our assets if it came down to it. We would do our best to help others in need, but our family comes first, because that's just how it goes.

Any situation of this caliber poses all kinds of problems that could arise. Sanitation issues would quickly become a top priority to avoid infections, illness and even death from poor sanitary conditions. A process for how to dispose of trash, feces and urine would be imperative. Having a way to keep clean hands, bodies and mouths would be crucial, too. We've yet to plan for how we'd handle these kinds of issues, but we definitely know they're important issues to consider.

At this point in the pyramid, we'd be seeking anything and everything that could give our children some sense of normalcy in a world that's been turned upside down. It would be such a life altering experience to go from living a life full of video games, TV and tablets to a life with no electricity, running water or trips to the grocery store. When we truly think about the possibilities these levels bring, it's more than daunting. We find peace in knowing that if such circumstances horrifically came to fruition, we'd undoubtedly do everything in our power to keep ourselves and our children as healthy and happy as we possibly can. That and we strongly believe that everything happens for a reason, so if we're brought to it, we'll find a way through it!

We hope that our perspective has brought you some awareness on the topic of prepping, if nothing else. We aren't expecting our world around us to collapse, but we hope the small steps we've made to prepare for the unknown will be enough to keep our family happy, healthy and alive regardless of any situation we may encounter. We hope that you use this book to its full potential. There is a plethora of pertinent information and resources for everyone from the "Minimal" prepper all the way to the "Off-the-Grid" prepper. Even if you don't consider yourself a prepper at all, this book offers so many tips on how to be more prepared than you are right now. Take advantage of this knowledge to safeguard you and your family from the possibility of any type of crisis or emergency situation that could occur. As the Boy Scouts of America always say, "Be prepared!"

*http://www.merriam-webster.com/dictionary/prepper (2/2013)
**http://en.wikipedia.org/wiki/Prepper (2/2013)
***http://www.urbandictionary.com/define.php?utf8=%E2%9C%93&term=prepper (2/2013)
**** http://www.power4patriots.com/ (2/2013)

Prepping for Seniors

By

Ken Clarke

Table of Contents

Chapter One

Remembering the past...

First, let's clarify what the definition of a Senior Prepper is and isn't. It's not about any specific age group, health issue, or lifestyle definition, it's about a way of life. Seniors don't all live in retirement homes, have grandkids, survive on a fixed income, or receive social security. They may live with their children or have grandkids living in their home. They may even still have a job, not that they need one, but because of the pleasure they get from still being part of a work force, being needed, able and willing to contribute. Many seniors have reached the point in life where satiability, security, family, and happiness are about equal in level and content but always subject to change. Seniors understand that life does have an end, time does go on, friends and family may pass but will never be forgotten.

Seniors also embrace history and knowledge. To me, seniors are a major archive of knowledge and the best teachers in the world. They are storehouses of the past and our best source for prepping in the future. They can tell us how life once was, and how it might someday be again. True seniors are ageless, timeless books that are just waiting to be read or re-read over and over throughout the course of their lifetimes. Just never count a senior out, while at the same time they are willing to teach, they have not forgotten their willingness to learn, as long as it's something new and if they can see the long term benefits of learning it.

Take my mother for example. At the age of seventy three she still has not grasped the concept of the internet, or smart phones. But each Christmas, holiday, and birthday, without fail, there is a card in my mailbox (*Notice I didn't say Inbox*) and each will have a small handwritten statement on the back of the envelope saying; "Don't open until" and the date. You might think this is old fashioned, but to me it reminds me that while e-mails might be quicker, and cheaper, they are also generic and lack a personal touch that says, "I still care and am thinking about you on this day." Lest we forget the wow factor; seeing the sparkle in your child's eyes when they open a card on their birthday and a pinch of glitter falls to the floor from inside the card.

For seniors, prepping isn't about learning something new, it's about remembering the past. A past, where shopping for grocery staples, more often than not, occurred once a month instead of once a week. Where your Mom might often be found in the kitchen canning the summer harvest, cooking a week's worth of food before freezing it, or writing down a new recipe before it pops out of her head. Dad might be out in the barn, working in the shed, battling weeds in the yard, milking cows, tending livestock or getting eggs from the chickens.

Seniors knew that electrical power was nice to have but the world still went on if it failed, and failures *always* occurred when you least expected them and might last for days or even weeks. Snow storms *always* occurred in the winter, they could be long, cold, and hard, and Dad always knew exactly how much firewood was needed and how long would it last. Seniors grew up during a time when everyone had fruit and nut trees in their yards, berry bushes around the edge, gardens in the back and roses in the front.

Apples not made into pies were always hung, dried, or canned, nuts gathered and stored, berries were canned, made into jams, jellies and preserves, or just packed into mason jars and preserved. Cucumbers were grown, pickles stored in brine, *(as were pigs feet, eggs and sausage)* and if a Senior lived on a farm; hogs were butchered and smoked, cattle was milked or slaughtered and turned into steaks and roast, chickens laid eggs until they couldn't lay anymore and then they were eaten. Crops were harvested, potatoes and carrots dug up, corn shucked, beans pulled and tomatoes eaten right off the vine. Their days started early, night came quick, and bedtime was shortly after nightfall because the early bird always got the worm.

Back then, in simpler times, radios were the most common form of entertainment followed by TV's that were watched, but only after the chores were done, *and,* if you were lucky, you might have gotten three different TV stations where you lived. Telephones were temperamental, cell phones didn't exist, and a quiet evening at home usually included a good book, a glass of milk, and a piece of homemade apple pie. Oh yea, books came from stores or the town library, not by downloading it to your iPad. The real fun started when the games were dug out, board *not* electronic, such as Monopoly, Chess, Parcheesi, Checkers and even plain old playing cards. Entertainment was a family adventure and something you looked forward to, not ran away from.

If you went further back in time, a mere sixty or seventy years ago, you might notice that the average home was a bastion for Preppers, designed for disaster preparedness, abnormal weather, environmental extremes, and acts of mother nature or wild animals. Bedrooms had extra blankets and pillows for the loss of power or unusually cold nights where it cost less to throw on another blanket than it did to turn the thermostat up. Every room, including the bathroom, had candles or oil lamps just in case the power failed, or heaven forbid if you wanted a romantic moment. Pantries were overstocked with canned foods, Mason jars of vegetables and fruits, meats and dried goods. Moms prepared for winter, the unexpected, or even just because she could. She didn't need a reason to prepare; she did it because her mother taught her and her mother before that. Self-reliance was the way of world, as there was not a superstore on every corner, so communities relied on themselves. More often than not, the food would be eaten before it went bad, or it might be traded for something your neighbor had that you didn't. Some families might even set a stand up on the edge of the road, with excess jars of jams and preserves, to sell what they didn't need. Even then, when company showed up for dinner or just to chat, the jars came out and were proudly passed around, and nobody left empty handed. I have been fortunate enough to visit the homes of Seniors who can pull down a mason jar or two and will proudly tell you that they might have been canned 10 or fifteen years ago but will taste just as good as the day they were sealed. Back then there was some type of magic used in the canning process. Something our grandmothers or great-grandmothers knew, that allowed anything stored in Mason jars to last a lifetime. *(If only Smuckers could patent that.)*

In addition, almost every farm had a storm shelter or just a really big below ground pantry. Our forefathers, or foremothers if you prefer, knew that storing things below ground kept them at a constant temperature and steady humidity. Root crops, also known as tubers, like potatoes, beets, yams, carrots, sweet potatoes, and others, can last for months or through a full winter underground. Today underground pantries are only used by Preppers, Survivalist, and or those wild and adventurous enough to challenge the great white north called Alaska.

In some cases, smoking was a great way to preserve fish and game for long term storage. Smoking provides meat with natural flavoring and removes the moisture that often causes meat to rot within days. Today you might have a dehydrator in your kitchen and use it to make dried fruits or beef jerky but our ancestors would use the same principle to preserve a few hundred pounds of fish, pork, venison, or beef. Our great grandparents knew how much food they needed to survive through a winter, a dry season, failed crops, or when times were just tough.

As our grandparents families grew, and the general population exploded, their children moved off the farms and into cities and suburbs. Places where the lessons of farm life were forgotten or just ignored. Grocery stores were convenient, neighbors were just right next door, not five miles down the road. Cities provided a place where children could grow up with the same friends and neighbors, find a sweetheart, date, and even get married, all within the same neighborhood, traveling less than five miles. Back yards might contain small gardens and window planters sometimes had spices, not flowers, and a farmer's market might just be right down the road, but having a full garden or livestock was no longer feasible, or allowed.

Block parties were popular, neighbors helpful when things got bad, and a cup of sugar might turn into a cup of coffee over the kitchen table or another friend for life. New neighbors were common, but welcomed with open arms and a potluck supper. Thus making the adjustment of a new home only as hard as remembering what Tupperware container or casserole dish belonged to whom, but the country way of life of preparing was soon forgotten.

Today, Senior Preppers have an advantage that younger Preppers don't; which is experience. Seniors still need to prepare for disasters or emergencies just like the rest of us, as it's a fact that disasters *still* occur, emergencies *still* happen and believe it or not, Mother Nature *still* throws us a curve ball every now and then. Senior Preppers need to accept that becoming a Prepper involves more than just gathering supplies, it means gathering knowledge, getting training, and accepting the fact that there may come the time where the safety and security of your family will become your responsibility.

The five mantras of a Prepper:

- ☐ Be educated, never stop learning.
- ☐ Have the attitude, but never be un-willing to change.
- ☐ Preparation takes time, effort, and thought. Never give up.
- ☐ Six "P's": Prior Planning Prevents Piss Poor Performance.
- ☐ Be willing to do whatever it takes to ensure your family's survival.

Chapter Two

Have a plan...

Senior Preppers need to start by making a plan. Plan on how much money you're willing to spend, how long you want your supplies to last, where you're going to Bug In at and where you're going to Bug Out. Plan on what emergency supplies you need, where you're going to store them, how you're going to transport them and where you're going to evacuate too. Build it in stages, write it down, draw a map, and then re-write it again. Plans can also be stored in your mind but if your mind is like mine, ah, what were we talking about?

A big consideration for most seniors is "Can I do this alone?" This is a major consideration and should not be considered lightly. If family or friends are close by, then they should become an integral part of your planning, and you should plan together as a team. If there are no close family or friends you could count on, consider joining a Preppers group. Preppers groups are like-minded people who band together to form a team and share ideas, resources and often plan on Bugging In or Out together as a team.

You might ask yourself, "What would a Preppers group want with some old geezer like me?" Well that answer is clear and obvious. **Knowledge and experience**. While other members may bring brawn, or technical skills to the table, I can guarantee that there are not too many twenty some things that know a lot about a simple internal combustion engine, how to work a pressure cooker, or how to sew on a trundle sewing machine or other skills that you bring to the table.

Don't count out your life experiences as not having value. I can recount many times that my Grandfather, who was 98 when he died, saved the day with some simple tried and true tested piece of advice to solve a problem that came straight from his life experiences.

Don't be afraid to think outside the box when looking for a Preppers group also. Often college aged, or newly graduated individuals have a Prepper Mentality, but don't have the finances or quite frankly take the time to do the planning involved. If you offer to perform the mental aspects of planning and organization, this is most likely the task that twenty some things are not willing to devote their time to and therefore would love for someone else to take on those chores.

Start with where you live...

To start off, you have to put yourself in the mind of a criminal. Start on the outside of your house. Take a full 360 degree set of photos and store them on your computer or laptop. At the same time go to Google Earth or your favorite mapping program and download a picture of your house. Examine your photos for blind spots. Places where a criminal cannot be seen from the street, areas where security lights don't cover, check access points to your home, windows hidden by bushes. Find any problems, and then fix them. Now go to each window and door on the inside of your home, and take a picture of what you see. Examine what's there for potential weak spots, blind spots or places that would allow someone to hide and watch you. You might even consider going out in your yard, to the edge of your property or even outside it and take photos at points where people can look in at you and your family. These are your areas of your least control, your weakest point. Gather all your information together, print it all out, put it in a binder along with your floor plans, property plans, and then print it all out. With this binder you can create defensive plans or bug out route as well as knowing where your blind spots are.

Examine your needs...

Prepping requirements vary greatly from a single healthy adult, to a family of two adults with five kids, but there are basic minimums that everyone needs to survive. Without these basic needs, your survival is never guaranteed and your survival will be dependent on others. They are: food, water, heat, security, habitation, transportation, safety, and hope.

- ☐ Food: A minimum of 1200 kcals *(defined as kilogram calories)* of food per person per day for a static or Bug In preparedness.

- ☐ Water: For someone who is going to be static, not working or walking in any form, the American Red Cross and FEMA state that you can survive on a minimum of 12 ounces of potable water *(defined as safe for drinking)* per person, per day. My personal recommendation is to maintain complete hydration for as long as possible until the need to ration water arrives. Additionally, a minimum of one gallon of gray water *(defined as untreated or unsafe water)*.

- ☐ Security: The ability to defend yourself from danger and provide protection for your family. Additionally, security involves keeping your environment and supplies safe and secure as well.

- ☐ Habitation: Keeping a roof over your head, whether it's a five thousand square foot home or a tent in the woods.

- ☐ Transportation: The ability to move from point A to point B. A vehicle, ATV, golf cart, bike or just your own two feet.

- ☐ Hope: Having the ability to believe in yourself, and that you can handle anything that comes your way without being dependent on the government or others. Your belief that you can do whatever it takes to ensure the safety and survival of your family.

Examine your environment...

For any age Prepper, you need to examine the environment you live in. Whether you live in a city center, metro suburbs, urban sprawl, rural, country or farm, each environment has special needs or requirements that Preppers must prepare for. Let's call them zones, zone one through zone four. They range from the center of a major metropolitan city, to a country home, farm, or hunting cabin in the woods. With each zone, there are different levels of concern as the more modern the environment you live in, the more dependent on modern conveniences you might have become.

Living in a city, hunting for food is as easy as walking to the local Chinese restaurant and getting an order to go. That is, until the restaurant closes due to lack of food to prepare, lack of electricity, etc. So, pulling out a rifle, finding a tree to climb or tall building to shoot from, will probably get you labeled a terrorist and you will more than not be spending your free time answering questions from the local FBI or Homeland Security. Not to mention there will not be much prey to be shooting at other than other humans and domesticated animals, and hopefully your situation does not come to that. The same goes for living within the city limits of a small suburban town. You might get away with it the first time but somebody in a home nearby will probably call the police and report you for shooting at domesticated animals. That's when the real trouble begins: your weapons could be confiscated, you run the risk of a criminal record, and you might even find your mug shot hanging on the wall of your local ASPCA. Worse, someone might start a Facebook page about you, and your name, address, and criminal history will be posted all over the internet, if the internet has survived.

These are the definitions of Zone One through Zone Four. Each has different concerns and different requirements for Prepping, Bugging in, and Bugging out.

Zone One:

Zone one is defined as a major downtown city or population center consisting of approximately one million or more residents. It can also be considered the center of a bull's-eye, or some of the most unsafe places to live during disasters or civil unrest.

In the case of most economical, environmental, or man-made disasters, city centers will be the first to be targeted, the first to lose control of its infrastructure, the first to run out of emergency and medical supplies, the most likely to lose power, water or food, and the most likely starting point of civil unrest. If you live in this zone, take a look at the history of where you live, where the safest residential zones are, what parts of your city have been deemed safe or unsafe by your fellow residents and local law enforcement.

Regardless of where in the city you live, Zone One seniors should never consider the option of staying in place or "Bugging In", but should always be prepared to immediately "Bug Out" or evacuate. Unfortunately, living in a Zone One environment may be comfortable and offer conveniences, but it's never safe. In cities, crime rates will become abnormally high during times of stress, storage space is extremely low, and the population per square mile always exceeds the ability of law enforcement to protect. Let's take the city of Atlanta Georgia for example; having a footprint of almost one hundred fourteen square miles, Atlanta piles in almost thirty two hundred residents per square mile, giving each resident less than two tenths of an acre per person. Even New York City is lower with a city footprint of over forty seven thousand square miles, and a mere four hundred twelve residents per mile, giving each resident a footprint of over six tenths of an acre. A Zone One population center may be one of the worst places to live in terms of a preparedness standpoint, but, if it is your choice, and you're willing to take the extreme measures to prepare, there are ways to ensure your survival.

First, accept the fact that where you live, in an apartment, condo, townhouse or in town home, may require physical reinforcement to insure you and your family's survival in case of a disaster or emergency. Examine the floor plan of your home for weak points, walls that can be breached by force with something as simple as a hammer or rock. Check the sturdiness of your door; is it steel, solid wood, or hollow core? What about the walls on each side of your door? Could someone kick a hole in the wall and reach through to reach your door lock? Is your door made of steel but your doorframe made of wood? What steps can you take to reinforce your door? Can you install slide bolts to your door to prevent it from being kicked in? Even something as simple as a few wood wedges and a hammer can lock your door firmly in place and prevent it from being kicked in or at least giving you enough warning time to prepare and defend yourself.

If your home is in a multistory building, can you physically maneuver yourself and family up and down stairs to access your home and the outside world. In bugging out, can you move your family and all your supplies to your vehicle? Is your home located close enough to the ground floor that someone could scale the exterior and have access to your windows or balcony, and thus gain access to your home? Can you use a window or balcony as a means of escape should your primary access be blocked or compromised?

Where is your vehicle located? Is it in an underground or above ground storage facility? What would happen to where your vehicle is stored if the power failed? Would the security gates be locked and access to your vehicle prevented? Would there be flooding in your parking structure during a storm?

Now consider where you're going to store emergency supplies. Does your home have enough available space for at least 30 days' worth of supplies? Do you have additional storage space in the basement of your building and again, can you gain access to it if the power fails? Does your complex or building have electronic door locks on your doors, parking, storage, stairwells, or front door access points?

Now let's talk about water. Humans can survive 30 days without food, but only three days without water. Some apartments or condominiums might have a limited amount of water stored on the roof or upper floors, but most modern building structures only operate on a booster pump system. These pumps are designed to boost water from the ground floor to the top floors then distribute it through the plumbing and sprinkler systems. Even if your building has backup generators, they will only work as long as their fuel supply lasts. Also, backup generators and booster pumps will only work if the city water supply remains flowing and untainted. With the failure of your buildings water supply, you also need to consider the failure of your home's fire sprinkler system. Fire sprinklers are a closed loop system that are designed to work even if the local water pressure fails, as the sprinkler system will contain water, under pressure, until the system is activated. Once activated, unfortunately, the water contained in a fire riser and sprinkler system is tainted and un-drinkable as the interiors of the steel pipes are treated to prevent rust. Once your main water supply fails, a sprinkler system may activate when a fire starts, but will fail when there is no additional water to fill the pipes. Even if the fire system has water, it may not have enough to completely put out a fire without additional water supply, therefore leaving your home vulnerable in either respect.

What about power? Does your building have backup generators? Where are they located? Many are located in basements, which can become flooded or be breached by outsiders to steal the fuel for their own uses. How long will they last? Knowing the complete details of your buildings maintenance lifelines will improve your survival and escape options. Explore those escape options, locate emergency accesses, stairwells, and exits. Create a plan, and then create a secondary plan. Test those plans, and then test them again with your entire family and be sure to include contingencies for someone being away from home. Figure out how you're going to evacuate, in the dark, without power, how you're going to get from where you live, to the ground floor, then to your vehicle. Learn, practice, then do it again, and again to ensure your survival.

Zone Two:

Populations within one to three miles outside a major city or population center are defined as what most people call "City sprawl". Residents in this area live in townhomes, apartments, condominiums, retirement homes, and small to medium sized homes on small lots. Some properties will have trees and are within a short commute to offices located in the downtown city area.

Preppers living in this area are still living in an area considered unsafe, but have the option of evaluating disasters to determine if Bugging Out is actually a necessity. Prepping in a Level Two zone must contain both elements of a Bug In and a Bug Out mentality and having plans in place for both options. Having both options will ensure that you cover all the bases whether situations are minor or things escalate out of control and the need to Bug Out becomes a necessity.

Again as in a Zone One, your first concern should be security. Where you live, an apartment, condo, or home, may require reinforcement to insure your survival in case of a disaster or emergency. First, examine where you live with maps and aerial photography. Use Google Earth or other mapping sites to print out detailed maps of your home and the surrounding area. Print both surface maps that show detailed road names and satellite photos that can show you ground paths that you might be able to use. Do you live in a gated community? Can the gate be manually opened should the power fail? Does your community or complex have a private security service? Will they remain in place should civil unrest occur in your area? Who can you depend on in your neighborhood? Are there others in your community that feel as you do towards Prepping? Create your own Prepping Group in your area to combine knowledge, skills and even resources.

Second, get a property plat of your home. Plats and blueprints to your home can be found in your city's planning office. For a small fee you can have a copy of your blueprints printed out and then laminated at a local Printing Center. Examine the floor plans of your home for weak points, walls that can be breached by force with something as simple as a hammer or rock. Ground floor windows and doors can also be weak points so consider purchasing a stock of sheet plywood and two by fours to cover ground floor windows and doors. Check the sturdiness of your doors; consider replacing standard doors with steel core or solid wood doors. Install additional door locks, braces, or even sliding bolts to strengthen your doors to prevent them from being kicked in. If your home has a garage, don't forget to reinforce the door between your home and your garage. If you live in an apartment or condo, are you located on or near the ground floor where someone might be able to scale the outside of your building to gain access to your home?

Where is your vehicle located? Is it in an underground or above ground storage facility? If your vehicle is parked in a garage, do you know how to open your garage door if the power should fail? If your vehicle is parked in an underground parking structure, would the security gates be locked and access to your vehicle prevented? Could there be flooding in your parking structure during a storm? Can you physically move your family and supplies to the location of your vehicle without the help of elevators which will be out of service?

Check with your local utilities company to find out where your source of water originates from. If it comes from a gravity fed water tower, remember that it takes power to fill that tower and once the power fails, eventually your supply of water will fail as well. If your water is supplied by a booster pump station, your water supply will be cut off when the power grid fails. Some booster stations have backup power supplies, but again, with time, the power will fail and water will dry up.

Finally, don't forget to make a bug out plan that includes getting from your home to your final bug out destination. Involve your family, children, and relatives in your plan so that they know where you're going to go and how you're going to get there. Plan for contingences such as someone not being at home when something happens, and how and where you would meet.

Zone Three:

Preppers in Zone Three live in small to medium cities that are between five to twenty miles outside the city center, consisting of suburbs, small cities, or unincorporated areas. Family homes may be in communities as large as 1000 homes on quarter acre lots, to as big as single family homes on one to ten acres. Your home may be on a public sewer system or a septic tank. You may have city water or have it pumped up from a well. Stores stay open late, crime statistics are low, convenience stores are open twenty four hours a day crime statistics don't dictate things like bars on your windows and doors. You might even be considered abnormal if you don't have trees in your front *and* back yard. Most residents work within the community or commute to the downtown area for employment.

Living in this area is still considered mildly unsafe but it doesn't mean that you need to consider immediate evacuation as your only option. It is recommended that you still make bug out plans, but when disasters occur, evaluate what possible dangers you might get caught up in if you Bug In, vs. what safety you might find by Bugging Out. Prepping in Zone Three should contain both elements of a Bug In and a Bug Out mentality and having plans in place for both options. Having both options will ensure that you cover everything, whether situations are minor or things escalate out of control.

Again, as in Zone One and Two, your primary concern should be security. The environment you live in, the home you own and the property that surrounds it may require reinforcement to insure your survival in case of a disaster or emergency.

First, examine where you live with maps and aerial photography. Use Google Earth or other mapping sites to print out detailed maps of your home and the surrounding area. Print both surface maps that show detailed road names and satellite photos that can show you ground paths that you might be able to use. Do you live in a gated community? Can the gate be manually opened should the power fail? Does your community or complex have a private security service? Will they remain in place should civil unrest occur in your area? Who can you depend on in your neighborhood? Are there others in your community that feels as you do towards Prepping? Create your own Prepping Group in your area to combine knowledge, skills and even resources.

Second, get a property plat of your home. Plats and blueprints to your home can be found in your city's planning office. For a small fee you can have a copy of your blueprints printed out and then laminated at a local Printing Center. Examine the floor plans of your home for weak points, walls that can be breached by force with something as simple as a hammer or rock. Ground floor windows and doors can also be weak points so consider purchasing a stock of sheet plywood and two by fours to cover ground floor windows and doors.

Check the sturdiness of your doors; consider replacing standard doors with steel core or solid wood doors. Install additional door locks, braces, or even sliding bolts to strengthen your doors to prevent them from being kicked in. If you home has a garage don't forget to reinforce the door between your home and your garage. If you live in an apartment or condo, are you located on or near the ground floor where someone might be able to scale the outside of your building to gain access to your home?

In this zone, most vehicles will be parked in driveways, on the street, or single dwelling garages. If you live in a home with an attached garage do you know how to open your garage door if the power should fail? Check with your local utility company to find out where your source of water originates from. If it comes from a gravity fed water tower, remember that it takes power to fill that tower and once the power fails, eventually your supply of water will fail as well. If your water is supplied by a booster pump station, your water supply will be cut off when the power grid fails. Some booster stations have backup power supplies but again, with time, the power will fail and water will dry up.

Zone Four:

Zone Four is neither clearly defined nor clearly marked. Starting at about 20 miles outside a major city center, it can go as far as fifty miles or even one hundred. It's a place where you feel safe and your need for staying in place outweighs your need to Bug Out. It's a place where others, your friends and family, will gather together to survive with you. You might have between five and 500 acres of land, your own lake or fresh water stream, perhaps your home can't be seen from the road, and your neighbors may be close, but still live a few miles away.

Your home may be new, or built by your ancestors and passed down. The power and telephone come in by pole, and you most likely have well water and your own septic tank. You have a fireplace that can actually heat your home and sometimes, in northern climates you have a wood burning stove and enough wood out back to last all winter if needed. You might cook with gas, but you always try to keep your propane tank at least three quarters the way full during the fall just in case of a winter storm.

Pantries are often below ground and so are storm shelters if they are not one in the same. Wherever they are, more often than not they are stocked with canned goods, dried meats, and dried fruits and vegetables. Oil lamps and candles abound, closets are full of quilts and blankets, and since children often have grown and moved away, you have more room than you need but it's always nice to have when the grandkids come for a visit. Zone four prepping isn't learning something new, it's about remembering something old. Remembering how to live off the land through farming, livestock or when needed, going out and gathering some meat the old fashioned way.

For Senior Preppers, this is where you make your last stand. If the power fails, you make your own or do without. If the water fails, you get a bucket or pump it by hand. Everyone helps each other, neighbors stand together, family comes home and friends stand together and pitch in to help one another.

Retirement or assisted living homes…

We all make choices in our lives; sometimes those choices are made for us when our daily life and health care become a burden on our husbands or wives, and in some cases, on our families. Being a resident of an assisted living or retirement home doesn't mean you can't be a prepper, as a matter of fact, it's a necessity to ensure your survival should some type of disaster occur.

First, you need to understand the mentality of those whom your care is dependent on. Most are not registered nurses or doctors but are just paid hourly employees of the company that owns the building you live in. And trust me, they are not being paid extravagant wages for the work they do. They will also have families of their own so should a disaster occur, and their families will become their first priorities *before* you and your care.

Those employees working at the time a disaster occurs will probably remain until the end of their shift, but when the oncoming shift fails to show to replace them, a few employees might remain for a time but eventually, they are going to slowly trickle away as they realize their responsibility to their children or families. I wouldn't blame them, I could even understand their wanting to be with their families, but even being sympathetic doesn't make it right when your care is being put at risk. Doctors and registered nurses may stay the longest as their Hippocratic Oath demands they stay and care for you, but it's hard to predict the actions of medical professionals when things seem hopeless.

For those whom have family members in retirement or assisted living homes you should take the time to speak with that family member and broach the subject of their wishes should a disaster occur. Would they want to remain in place or would they want to be Bugged Out? In some cases they may not be able of making that choice. If you don't have a power of attorney or they have a directive that specifically covers their wishes should something occur, the decision to help may be completely out of your hands. If that is the case, you can take some steps to ensure the survival of your relative or family member until the situation gets out of control and you have no choice but to attempt their recovery.

Survival preparations:
- ☐ The next time you visit your relative; start asking questions about your family member's diet and nutritional requirements. Find out how they are fed, through standard meals or through a gastro intestinal tube. If they are on a solid food diet, consider bringing a case of emergency food rations like MRE's that don't require cooking, ration bars, if they are able to chew solid foods, or liquid protein supplements like Ensure if they are on a liquid

diet. Help keep them supplied with a weeks' worth of additional food above and beyond their daily requirements. Additionally, keep a well-stocked supply at your home if you intend on bringing your relative or family member home in an emergency.

☐ Ask about your family members medical requirements. Check what type of prescriptions they are on and if it's possible for you to retain some of their medication in your home should you have to pick up your family member and bring them to your home. Never forget to pick up any remaining prescriptions when you pick up your family member. If possible, speak to your family member's physician and request a supply of their prescriptions be filled and left at your home.

☐ Does your family member require oxygen? Consider purchasing a small home oxygen generator or bottled oxygen. Remember to purchase regulators, hoses, masks, or nasal cannula equipment, and have it stored at your home just in case it's needed.

☐ Make sure your family member has one week worth of clothing on hand in their room as well as extra things like adult diapers, hand lotion, hand sanitizer, shoes, and a cell phone. Supply their room with a stock of bottled water should local water supplies fail.

☐ Supply them with a basic Bug Out kit or bag that contains things like a flashlight, matches, candles, Mylar blanket, vitamins a small battery powered AM/FM weather radio, personal hygiene supplies, and a basic plan that tells them where you should meet if their building is damaged or destroyed, what numbers to call in case of emergency, and other emergency instructions.

☐ When you have to Bug Out a relative or family member that can't get out on their own, don't wait until the last minute, make it the first thing you do. Your family members are depending on you for their ultimate survival, so don't forget to remember them.

Making a Bug Out plan...

Create an evacuation plan that doesn't just include getting out of your residence, but out of your city as well. Build it in stages, and draw a map, or write it down.

☐ From your home to your vehicle: If you live in an apartment, always plan on taking the stairs when it's time to bug out. Even if the power is on, you don't want to get stuck in an elevator should the power fail during your Bug Out. Make plans to move your Bug Out supplies with you. Do you have a cart or dolly, a perhaps a winch or other means of lowering supplies from a window to the ground floor.

☐ From your vehicle to the city limits. Expecting to be alone on the roads during a disaster is a huge mistake. Believe me when I say that even if you're the first to Bug Out, you won't be on the roads alone. Plan on taking secondary roads and get a paper map in case electronic devices are no longer working. With the loss of power, expect cell phone towers to fail and with them, your GPS mapping program.

☐ From the city limits to the suburbs. Once out of the city, stick to secondary roads and off the main evacuation routes. Find a primary Bug Out location at a friend or family member's home in a rural area and map your route there. Let them know in advance of your plans so that you're not arriving at their doorstep without some warning. Remember that if the situation is bad enough, where you're going might only be as safe as your ability to prepare will allow.

☐ From the suburbs to beyond: Create a list of alternative or secondary bug out locations that will take you further and further away from the city. A relative's home, a secondary house, hunting cabin, or just somewhere rural. Calculate how far you can get on one tank of gas, and then subtract 25%. Gather where others might meet you to create a secure location for your friends and family to gather.

☐ List addresses, names, and numbers, of the destinations of your Bug Out plans. Write it up, and then pass it out. Let your family know of your plans so that there is less stress on them should you be out of communications for a short time. Make hard copies, laminate it and snail mail it to those who need to be in the know.

☐ Stick to the plan whenever possible. If you stray from your plan, or have problems, like having to take alternative routes due to traffic and safety issues, you may make it more difficult for others to find you if you fail to show.

☐ Give reasonable time estimates but don't forget to allow for the anything can A. C. H. effect. (Anything Can Happen) Take the time you expect to travel from point A to Point B and figure in items such as traffic signals being out, bridges may be out and roads impassable in natural disasters, etc. It is more important that loved ones know your intended routes and alternates than actual time estimates, as those may vary based on many factors.

Chapter Three

First there was camping...

In the beginning, man created fire. Well, God created fire and man just took the credit for it. But man did invent camping. Actually, man was camping before he invented traditional housing, but let's not argue that point right now. The point I'm trying to make is that as a part of prepping, you have to discuss camping. The reason is that prepping is just like getting ready for a long camping trip, a real long camping trip.

Like prepping, camping supplies are the same supplies you would want to have with you for disaster preparedness. The definition of camping can vary from person to person, some like to define camping as "Roughing It"; Packing it in, and only taking what you can carry on your back. The opposite end of the spectrum might be called "Glamping"; Defined as driving in a two hundred thousand dollar RV, sleeping in an air conditioned room, on a real bed with a real toilet, full kitchen and satellite TV on a flat screen that would make any American male proud. Now "Glamping" is not my definition of camping, but to each their own. There is however, no doubt that having a standard supply of camping gear as the starting point for your prepping supplies is a first step[on becoming prepared. The following list contains what an average family of four, two adults and two children, would normally, or should normally, take with them on short camping trip.

- ☐ At a minimum, a four-person tent should suffice but check the cost of a six-person tent and if the difference in price is negligible, get a six-man tent as you're going to want the extra room to store supplies.

- ☐ One sleeping bag for each member of your family. Don't buy children's sleeping bags if you have children, buy adult bags and roll them up if they are too long. As your children grow, they will grow into their bags.

- ☐ Two, 20 by 20 foot, heavy duty tarps. One for putting under your tent, one for putting over your tent or over your campsite.

- ☐ Air mattress or foam pads. Not an extreme necessity, but nice to have if you have the space. Often seniors find cots easier to get into and out of, and many have mattresses attached or available.

- ☐ Four folding chairs. Again don't buy children size chairs, buy adult size chairs that your children can grow into over their lifetime.

- ☐ A folding or camp table. Like folding chairs you should be able to find one that folds up and can be carried over your shoulder.

- ☐ AM/FM weather radio.

- ☐ A true GPS, not a cell phone with GPS. Remember cell phone GPS's will not function without cell service as that is how it downloads the maps of the area you're in.

- ☐ Gas or fuel oil powered lantern.

- [ ] Gas or propane powered two burner camp stove. Additionally, you're going to want to pack pots, pans, spatulas, serving spoons, plates, forks, knives (eating and cutting), a cutting board, bowls, soap, dishwashing liquid, salt pepper, oil, sugar, dish towels, scrubbers, sponges, hot pads, spices, aluminum foil, etc.

- [ ] 100 feet of braided Polly rope with a test strength greater than the weight of your heaviest family member.

- [ ] 100 to 200 feet of nylon parachute cord (paracord).

- [ ] Four battery powered flashlights and spare batteries.

- [ ] Each person will need to bring a backpack with a change of clothes for every two days of your trip. Bring extra socks and underwear along with a sweater or jacket even if you think the weather doesn't require it. Toothbrush, toothpaste, dental floss, bug spray, shampoo, bar of soap, comb or brush a small towel (sponge towel) and hand cloth.

- [ ] Each person should bring the contents of their own bug out bag. Check the chapter on "Bug Out Bags" for the recommended contents.

Chapter Four

Creating your own survival food...

Survival food can be purchased premade or you can learn the skills needed to make your own. Canning, a tried and true technic for long term food storage, can be learned from those who still do it or from a book you pick up at your local library. Trust me when I say canning isn't hard to learn as long as you remember one word, "pasteurization".

Canning pasteurization is the process of heating food prior to or after you put it into Mason jars, heating it up in a pot full of boiling water or a steam bath, capping it, then once it comes up to temperature, remove it from the heat and immediately cool it by plunging it in ice water so that as the product cools, and a vacuum is created. Home grown, fresh vegetables are perfect for canning as you can take a normal shelf life of a few weeks and extend it to a few years. Pasteurization also works well on meats like chicken, pork, and beef, by precooking the meat, *(Parboiling it is preferred)* removing any bones, packing the meat in mason jars, pouring in the grease and drippings, heating it up to temperature, capping it, then once it comes up to temperature, remove it from the heat and immediately cool it by plunging it in ice water. Canning jams, jellies, and preserves are a little harder as it requires cooking and creating the preserves first before going through the whole pasteurization process to prepare it for long term storage.

Smoking, also called dehydrating, is another way of preserving food for long term storage and is again a step that can be learned from others or through knowledge contained in books. Dehydrating is a simple process of taking raw meat and cooking it by heating it until all the moisture is removed. With dehydrating you can pre-season your meat to create flavored jerky, or just dehydrate it for vacuum sealed storage. Dehydration can also be used to preserve fruits and vegetables that would only last days or weeks in a refrigerator, but will last years when dried. One thing to remember is that when you are dehydrating fruit like bananas or strawberries, you need to keep the thickness of your slices to about a quarter of an inch and as evenly sliced as possible so that the moisture levels in each slice are the same and the drying time will be equal. Once your fruit is dehydrated, and the same with your meats as well, the sooner you get it into a vacuum sealed bag the longer it will last as even dehydrated foods will spoil with time and oxygen.

Another means of creating long term storage food supplies is vacuum sealing. It's a process of removing as much if not all of the oxygen from previously dried product like grains, beans, rice, and pasta through the use of a vacuum powered device. With vacuum sealing, you can purchase food staples in bulk, such as a twenty five pound sack of rice, breaking it down to more manageable amounts that will be consumed in a reasonable amount of time, then putting it into Food-safe or Mylar bags. Unfortunately, even with vacuum sealing, you're not removing 100% of the oxygen. The air we breathe contains more than 78% nitrogen, 20% oxygen, 0.93% argon, 0.039% carbon dioxide, and small amounts of other gases, so once you vacuum seal the container, it still contains 20% oxygen, even in minute amounts. Once sealed, the rice has a shelf life of a few months but it can be extended by inserting an oxygen absorbing device in your bag prior to vacuum sealing it.

Oxygen Absorbers are small fiber or cloth pouches about the size of a sugar packet that contain a material called powdered iron, or iron salts. Powdered iron, when it comes in contact with oxygen, basically absorbs the oxygen and turns to rust. With this absorption, as a byproduct, heat is generated. Iron salts, on the other hand, are designed as heat generators, and come with the byproduct of absorbing oxygen. Both work quite well as oxygen absorbers, are non-toxic and food safe, and are a low cost alternative for the long term storage of food products. When combined with vacuum sealing, you not only remove as much air as possible, what remains is 100% oxygen free and almost pure nitrogen in content.

Then there is our next type of storage called "nitrogen flush". Nitrogen flush is popular with those who pack large quantity supplies for long term storage like dried corn, animal feed, dog or cat food, and grains like wheat and rye. Nitrogen can be used with smaller supplies but flushing only works best in an oxygen free environment. One of the best and most economical ways is to use a vacuum sealer inside a large tub. This tub will be filled with nitrogen, then you flush the contents of your Mylar or food saver bag with nitrogen, then seal them with heat all while still in the tub. This will insure that your survival foods only contain nitrogen. Nitrogen also works when you're sealing food in plastic containers or glass jars. Just put the hose into your container, turn on the gas and with the gas running, fill your container. Once your container is full, slowly pull the hose out until you can cap, cover or seal your container. Remember that as long as your container is sealed, it will remain nitrogen filled. Once you open it, oxygen will re-enter your container along with microbes and bacteria.

Another gas that can be used for prepping food for long term storage is carbon dioxide. In its gas form, it is heavier than air and will fill containers from the bottom up and replace the oxygen. I like to use it in its dry ice form, by getting a block of dry ice from your local grocery store. For a container smaller than one gallon, a piece about the size of the last knuckle of your thumb will do the trick. For containers that are between one and five gallons in size, use a piece of dry ice that is about the size of a golf ball. When filling containers larger than five gallons you're going to need piece of dry ice the size of a baseball. The great thing about dry ice is the fact that it converts from a solid to a gas without stopping or going into a "wet" or liquid stage. So it's perfect for storing dried goods like flour, corn starch, baking soda, or more! Remember; *never* secure the lid of your container until the ice has finished subliming from a solid to a gas. Sealing the container early can result in it exploding and breaking the seal.

Salting is also an old fashioned way of storing meats or fish for long term storage. Used by ships crossing the oceans for thousands of years, salting was a great way to extend the shelf life of dried fish and smoked meats by filling a barrel with salt and smoked meats. Unfortunately, once the barrels were opened, the fish would be exposed to moisture and its harmful friend, bacteria. Today barrels are no longer used but I always suggest the Preppers friend, snap lid storage containers. Start with a layer of salt on the bottom, then alternating with layers of meat, covered by layers of salt, meat, salt, etc. Your final layer should be salt and completely cover your meat from exposure. Finally, make your tub airtight by sealing it with tape, hot glue or caulk, and then pack it away for the future.

What you store your survival supplies in is as important as what you store inside. Any plastic food container that you can recycle should be food safe for long term storage as long as you can get an air tight seal. Two liter soda bottles are great for storing grains, rice and beans as long as you get the oxygen out of the bottle. Mason jars are great but never recycle the lids as once used they will start to dry out or can crack. Non recycled containers, purchased expressly for storing emergency food supplies, should be marked as food safe with a triangle on the bottom and the number two inside it. You can even purchase five gallon buckets from a local hardware store with snap on lids, just make sure they have that triangle, with the two in it, on the bottom. Mylar bags can be used as a buffer between your container and your food or you can store multiple smaller Mylar bags in a five gallon bucket. Fortunately, Mylar bags can be purchased in sizes as small as pints to as big as a fifty-five gallon drum.

Chapter Five

Purchasing Third party survival food...

There are many different companies that produce and sell Emergency Survival Food, in lots of shapes and varieties. Emergency food can come in meal bars, pouches of paste type food product, MRE's (Meals ready to Eat) or come as freeze dried and dehydrated either as single ingredient or combined into entrees.

Meal replacement bars are simple and will keep you alive, but might not appeal to your palate. MRE's are concise and a full meal, but often are bland, and are designed to be heated using the enclosed heat pouches or with boiling water. Taste testing and looking at the calorie count of these items is the best course of action to make a decision on whether or not they will suit your needs.

The last category is freeze dried and/or dehydrated foods. In this case, we are going to talk about combining entrée choices, not single ingredient as those are used to lay in stock for a large pantry, not immediate bug out purposes. Many freeze dried and/or dehydrated products come in cans or pouches, and some companies sell pouches bundled in four or five gallon buckets for storage and transport purposes. I can't tell you what brand to buy but what I can do is tell you exactly what to look for and what to avoid.

- ☐ First don't look for the highest number of servings you can find per container. The lower the number of servings per container, the more likely what you're getting is solid servings, not soups. You want to find containers of food that are at least 80% meals, like Beef Stroganoff, Chili Macaroni, Chicken Teriyaki and Rice, and others. The 20% soups per container are liquid nutrients that may taste good but won't give you that full feeling or carry as high a calorie count.

- ☐ Stay away from Emergency Food containers that contain Whey Milk. Some companies pad their content totals with 80 or 100 servings of Whey Milk but don't advertise clearly that the serving count includes whey milk. Others do not advertise clearly that their container only has soups, or a high percentage of soups, not solid meals.

- ☐ Remember that there are 100% vegetarian Emergency Food Supplies and 100% real meat Emergency Food supplies. Check the labels before you buy, and if you're buying off the internet, ask the seller to e-mail you a scan of the contents before you make any purchases.

- ☐ Vegetable based proteins in Emergency Food Supplies have a longer shelf life of between 20 and 40 years depending on how they are stored. Proteins of real meat can often be stored for up to ten years before they go bad. Trust me when I say that both vegetable based, and meat based proteins taste pretty good when it's all you have to eat.

- ☐ Look for companies that sell freeze dried meats, eggs, milk, vegetables, and fruits as supplements to normal meals. Also be sure to stock spices to liven up your food and make it more palatable.

☐ Always check the date of manufacture before you purchase your Emergency Food Supplies. If the seller assures you that it is current stock but can't show you the born on date, just walk away and buy it from someone else.

☐ Look at the serving size and the calories per serving. If you can't make 5 servings equal 1200 to 1500 calories, then you're going to need to add something to your meals to support your 1200 kcal minimum.

☐ Do a cost per calorie calculation when you find high quality emergency food suppliers you want to buy from. Do not use a cost per serving as calorie counts per serving can vary widely and you need a food supply to provide a set number of calories per day. Take the number of calories per serving then multiply it by the servings per container. Divide that number by the cost of the container to get a cost per calorie. Using this formula will give you a good cost per serving price that you can use to compare the value of the product you're anticipating purchasing.

☐ Medium shelf life Emergency food supplies (five to ten year shelf life) are great additions to your emergency food supplies but do not make them your main source as the short shelf life will triple or quadruple your cost when you have to replace it every five years. Again, check the born on date when you purchase your supplies as buying four year old product with a five year shelf life equals one year of remaining shelf life.

Chapter Six

Medicines and Mother Nature...

Seniors know, as we grow older, our body needs medicines and supplements to balance its needs and daily requirements to survive. Unfortunately, as we all know, when disasters occur, the possibility of medicines and supplements running out or being in short supply, becomes a reality. There are some simple steps you can take to insure your medicinal supplies don't run out or at least last through a disaster or emergency.

Please consult with your physician before taking any of this advice.

- Ask your Doctor to make all your prescriptions a 90 day supply. With generics your total cost per prescription should be around ten dollars. With non-generic prescriptions, check with the internet for the lowest prices you can find and then have your pharmacy price match.

- Ask your doctor to double your prescription size then split your pills. Again with generics it's not going to increase your prices just double your medications form 90 days to 180. With non-generic prescriptions, check with the internet for the lowest prices you can find and then have your pharmacy price match.

- With insurance, the date you can get a refill is determined by the insurance company. But that doesn't mean you can't get your prescriptions refilled up to seven days early. Continuing to do this will help you to gather a stockpile of your medicines in case something occurs and your medications run out.

- Consider alternative medicines for common ailments. Antibiotics can legally be purchased over the internet when used for pets. They are the exact same chemicals, in the exact same doses as your doctor prescribes, just without the fancy packaging and abnormal costs.

- Investigate homeopathic or alternative medicines for the prescriptions you are currently on. Not to replace the prescriptions you're currently on but as an alternative should your prescriptions run out in an emergency.

- Purchase and stockpile nutritional supplements like vitamins or minerals you take on a daily basis. Purchase a two year supply, then after you have used up your first years' worth, buy another year and continue to always rotate your stocks.

Chapter Seven

Storing your supplies…

Getting your supplies might just be the easiest part of prepping; finding places to store it could be the most difficult, and hopefully not cost you your marriage. This chapter will contain multiple options and it's your choice to pick and choose from them all.

Storing in your home…

While storing Emergency food supplies in your home keeps them close at hand, it's not always my first recommendation. Think of it this way: if your home is damaged in a disaster, tornado, forest fire, or civil unrest, then your survival supplies are going to be a big puddle of plastic mixed with debris or burning embers in what remains of your home. If you have no choice, and there are no alternatives, like those living in apartments or condo's, then make do with what room you have and be creative. High shelves in closets or top cabinets in kitchens can be used for storage and since you will not be accessing the items often the difficulty reaching them will not be as big an issue. Another area to consider is under your bed. If your bed is low to the floor, consider buying bed boosters, small blocks or pedestals you can put under the feet of your bed to bring its height up by several inches.

Consider your basement…

If you have a basement or crawl space, consider storing your emergency food supplies where your home is the coolest. Something that most manufacturers of emergency survival food will tell you, (*the reputable ones that is)*, is that the colder the temperature you store your supplies at, the longer you're your emergency food will last. Most manufactures recommend a maximum storage temperature of no higher than seventy-six degrees and out of direct sunlight. If your storage is between fifty-five and sixty-five degrees and you can add five to ten years to your emergency food supplies. Store it underground, in a pantry or cache and your twenty year supply of emergency food could last up to forty years.

Storing it outside of your home…

With those who have property, consider storing your emergency supplies outside your home like in a barn or a shed, but whenever possible, underground is the best recommendation I can make. If you have a shed, outbuilding, or even a dog house, move it out of the way, dig a hole big enough to store 6 months of emergency food, cover it with topsoil than put your shed back on top. What's that old saying? Out of sight, not out of mind? Besides if your house does burn down, or heaven forbid get sucked away by a twister, your emergency supplies will still be in place when you need them, not burnt or scattered across forty acres.

Get a trailer…

One thing I always suggest to Preppers is to consider storing your prepping supplies in a small automobile, truck or SUV trailer. You should be able to park it in your driveway, apartment's garage, or just keep it parked at a nearby storage facility. Do be mindful that it should not be parked in sunlight as this will damage your food supply and significantly shorten it's shelf life. An awning, simple shed or underground garage will protect it from the sun, and potential vandalism. Look for a single axle, one thousand to fifteen hundred pound towing weight trailer that would allow you to store camping and emergency supplies close at hand but instantly mobile in a disaster.

Additionally, make sure you park your trailer someplace where you can chain an axle or the hitch to a post or pipe. Never chain it to a pipe painted red as these are part of the fire sprinkler system and will probably result in your locks being cut and your trailer being towed. If not possible, run a chain through a wheel then back to the hitch or purchase a wheel lock system. Make sure to secure it with a heavy duty lock, something that is difficult if not impossible to cut. And *never* make the mistake of buying a really tough lock then using it on really cheap chain. Additionally, get a solid trailer ball lock and a hitch padlock. Then secure the trailer doors with a heavy duty padlock that is tamper resistant.

Along with your camping supplies, your trailer should also contain the following;

- ☐ A spare 12 volt car battery, charged.
- ☐ A small bottle jack, able to lift at least one ton.
- ☐ A spare tire stored inside the trailer to prevent it from being stolen.
- ☐ A 12 volt tire inflator and a can of Fix-A-Flat®.
- ☐ A small, gasoline powered, portable generator- in the 2000-kw range.
- ☐ A folding cart or wagon.
- ☐ 50 to 100 feet of grounded power cords and a surge strip.
- ☐ 10 to 20 feet of chain with padlocks.
- ☐ Between 10 and 20 gallons of gasoline that has been stabilized for long term storage.
- ☐ Twenty or thirty gallons of chlorinated or distilled water.
- ☐ One or two cases of bottled water.
- ☐ A water filtration device, funnel and pail.
- ☐ Fifty percent of your long term emergency food supplies.
- ☐ Several hundred feet of braided Polly rope with a test strength greater than your weight.
- ☐ Battery operated AM/FM/Weather radio.
- ☐ An empty backpack for each member of your family.
- ☐ Extra blankets and pillows.
- ☐ Flashlight and spare batteries.
- ☐ Electronic or chemical road flares.

- ☐ A machete and large belt knife.
- ☐ A small axe or hatchet.
- ☐ A bundle of pre-seasoned fire wood.
- ☐ Matches, lighters, and fire starters.
- ☐ A roll or two of duct tape.
- ☐ Roll of black and red electrical tape.
- ☐ Multi tool with wire cutters and knife.
- ☐ A roll of 3 mill thick black plastic sheeting.
- ☐ A box of heavy duty construction grade trash bags.
- ☐ An empty five gallon bucket, kitchen size trash bags and toilet paper.
- ☐ Folding shovel

Consider caching…

For those who have to Bug Out, Caching, or pre staging supplies can also be an option if you're limited on space in your vehicle or trailer. Once you have a pre-planned Bug Out route, find city, county, or state parks, vacant lots, or even rest areas on the side of the highway where staging a container of disaster supplies would be beneficial and could possibly save your life in an emergency. Caches should be pre-positioned every fifty to one hundred miles along your Bug Out route between your home and your finial destination.

Cache containers can be as large or as small as you want them but for most Preppers, twenty five to thirty gallon snap lid storage containers, preferably green in color, are the most commonly used. Fill the bottom of the cache container with about an inch of kitty litter then fill with your survival supplies. The kitty litter acts as a moisture absorber *and* will absorb any fuel that might leak from your gasoline supply. Including a moisture absorbing product like Damp-Rid®, will help to control moisture but *won't* do anything about spilled fuel or oil. Remember if done properly, your cache should last a minimum of ten years or longer so pack things carefully. If you're going to include gasoline, make sure it's treated with a gasoline stabilizer and that the container is safe for long term storage.

Same goes for storing water, in the fact that you're going to want to store it in BPH free containers, and something that is *not* biodegradable. Whatever container you use, make sure you store it with the cap up so that if it expands when frozen, the cap will pop off before the container ruptures. Additional supplies should be stored in airtight/watertight or vacuum sealed containers. When full, seal the lid to your cache in place with a bead of waterproof caulk. Then tape the lid down to let it dry. Drying times can vary with the type of caulk you use so just leave the tape in place when you bury your cache container. Remember, an airtight cache container will extend the life of your supplies, prevent any type of environmental exposure, and prevent moisture damage.

Reviews maps to find possible caching locations, then take a day trip to visit them and check out available sites. Don't forget to bring a shovel, pick, axe, hand saw, drop cloth or plastic sheet, and a flashlight. Make sure you take your cache containers with you so once you find a good site; you can put your cache in place. Typical cache sites will be under trees, in the middle of a group of bushes, or near a large pile of rocks. Find someplace that has easy access and can't be seen by a typical passerby. Then mark it with a large stone or branch and walk away. Continue walking around the site and see how visible it is from different locations and at different distances.

Once you have your site, prepare it by pulling away all loose ground cover until you reach packed dirt. Put a drop cloth down because by the time you finish digging your cache hole you're going to have more dirt then you will need and you're going to have to move it to prevent your cache from being identified. Dig your cache hole six to twelve inches deeper than you need so that there is limited risk of your water freezing. It will also help to know what the frost layer is in your area so that you know exactly how deep you need to dig.

If your cache location you've picked is under a tree, be prepared to cut the roots that may be in your way. Once you've dug the hole, place your cache in the hole and cover it with the dirt you dug from the hole then recover the site with the loose ground cover you removed before digging. Drag off any excess dirt you have and dispose it far enough away from your site so it isn't noticed. Finally, step back from where your cache is buried and examine the site for any signs you might have left behind. Erase shoeprints and scuff marks with a broken tree branch then pull out your map and mark the site of your cache on it. Some Preppers even take photos of their cache sites but there are no guarantees that the site will remain the same over time. Write down any details of your cache location and describe anything that may remain in place over time. Measure distances in steps from your cache to recognizable objects like rocks.

Caches should contain at least most of the following items, but are only limited to available space and your own imagination.

- ☐ A thirty day supply of emergency food or long term survival rations.
- ☐ Two or three gallons of gasoline that has been stabilized for long term storage.
- ☐ Two or three gallons of water.
- ☐ Mylar emergency blankets.
- ☐ One brown plastic 10 X 10 or larger tarp.
- ☐ 100 feet of braided nylon parachute cord in black, camo or brown.
- ☐ Matches, candles and fire starter. (Alcohol based hand sanitizer works great.)
- ☐ Some type of long knife or edged weapon.
- ☐ Flashlight and batteries.
- ☐ First Aid Kit
- ☐ Toilet Paper

☐ A roll of duct tape. *(It has so many uses I couldn't list them all here)*

Chapter Eight

Know what types of disasters...

No matter how you spell it, there are only two types of disasters. The first is natural or acts of Mother Nature, and the second being manmade.

Natural disasters:

- **Earthquakes:** Not much you can do about these except the obvious; don't live in an earthquake prone zone. Just say no and stay away from fault lines. If you have no choice, make sure your home has modern earthquake construction designs in effect like corner bracing, heavy duty anchor bolts, and sill plates.

- **Hurricanes:** Ocean born hurricane season occurs between June 1st and November 30th of each year. The Saffir–Simpson hurricane wind scale (SSHWS) rates hurricanes from a Category One (minimum 74 mph winds) to a Category Five (wind speeds greater than 157 mph), but the greatest damage comes from the storm surge, the rise of water surrounding the center of the storm. Fortunately, hurricanes come with advanced warning. We track them, follow their path, and can correctly predict, with some degree of certainty, the path they are going to take. The best way to avoid them is to not live on the coast. Trust me; they don't have hurricanes in South Dakota.

- **Tornados:** Unlike hurricanes, tornados are unpredictable and often come without warning. Tornados are only predictable in the fact that they occur more often in certain areas of the country, that they are likely to occur during certain times of the year, and they most often are created by super cell storms. Like hurricanes, tornados are rated on a scale from F0 to F5 on the Fujita scale. The Fujita scale is based on damage amounts not wind speeds as in most tornados wind speeds can vary from almost nothing at it's outer edges to well over 300 miles per hour at the center.

- **Extreme winter weather:** Take extremely cold weather, heavy snowfalls, and high winds, and you have trouble. Add in a power failure or loss of heat and things can go from extremely dangerous to downright deadly. This is where your camping gear can save your life. Put up a tent in your living room, roll out your sleeping bags, light your lamps, throw a log in your fireplace, and don't forget to drain your pipes!

- **Floods:** Again, naturally occurring, not much you can do to prevent them. But whenever possible, don't live on known flood plains. Love living on a river or near a lake? Get a houseboat or put your house on stilts. Keep plenty of plastic sheeting handy and if possible, have a gasoline powered pump on hand.

- **Tsunami or tidal waves:** An event that starts for many reasons, volcanic eruptions, seismic shifts, underwater landslides, or anything that causes massive shifting of mass or water. They can also be caused by the impact of meteorites into ocean waters. These waves can start as small waves in the depth of the ocean and crest hundreds of feet high when they hit the coast. The end result of this wall of water would be the extreme rise in coastal waters and the inundation of coastal cities and population centers. The effects would be short term but the damage would be extensive.

- **Coastal flooding:** Also an un-predictable, natural occurring event that can be caused by the melting of the polar ice, global warming, shifting of the poles or short term by large storms which push the sea inland. Coastal flooding can only be prevented by not living on the coast, and whenever possible, living at least 614 miles inland, and 1024 feet above sea level.

- **Volcanic eruption or super caldera:** Another time bomb, just waiting to go off. Eruptions occur without warning but on known fault lines, near known volcanic hot spots.

- **Forest Fires:** Combine dry heat, low moisture and some type of ignition, natural or man-made, and you get forest fires. Forest Fires can be as small as a brush fire or as large as a firestorm, burn as little as a few square acres or hundreds of square miles. The most often occur on the western half of the United States but can also occur in land that was never once considered fire prone. Forest Fires are extremely unpredictable and often come without warning or change unpredictably as winds can shift or weather conditions can accelerate them.

- **Solar flare or coronal mass discharge:** Again, out of man's control. If one of these occurs, there is not much you can do to prevent the damage and your going to have little if any warning. Light from the sun arrives on earth within 8 minutes so If you observed a massive solar flare or noticed the sun exploding out of the corner of your eye, remember it occurred about eight minutes ago and by the time you see it it's already too late.

- **Electromagnetic pulse:** Also created by the sun, it is a force of energy powerful enough to damage or destroy electronic devices across the face of the planet and if it continues longer then twelve hours, around the earth. Fortunately, if an EMP burst occurs and where you live is currently on the dark side, you might have a few hours to protect your electronics by removing the batteries and storing them in a Ferriday cage.

- **Asteroid or meteorite impact:** Hundreds of thousands of meteoroids or asteroids impact the earth in a year but fortunately for us, most are small enough so that they either burn up on entering our atmosphere or by the time they strike the earth they are the zie of a peanut. Compare that to the meteor which created the crater in Arizona, which was struck by a meteor approximately one hundred and fifty feet in diameter and traveling at twenty eight thousand miles an hour. The impact created a crater nearly one mile across, 2.4 miles in circumference and more than 550 feet deep. But what we, and our governments, are worried about is a meteorite greater than one mile in diameter that would cause an extinction level event and wipe out all life on the planet.

Man Made Disasters:

- **Economic:** This disaster can come in many different forms but all of them are based on money or its lack thereof. Even with preparation, everyone depends on our government to prevent economic collapse and unfortunately, as the past has shown us, sometimes the government is often the cause.

- **Political:** A political disaster revolves around our government's inability to work together for the benefit of the people. A political disaster can range from a budget filibuster causing a temporary shutdown, to an overthrow by domestic or foreign powers.

- **Civil**: Whether the result of race, religion, or political party, civil unrest often leads to civil war or the battle between the populations of different or similar parties. In America, our first civil war started because of our different beliefs in racial equality. In today's society, it would seem to be almost impossible for a similar civil war to occur yet they are occurring every day around the world.

- **Nuclear**: If you had asked me forty or fifty years ago, what the odds were of life as we know it ending in a Nuclear war I might have said somewhere around eighty percent. Today I don't expect death by nuclear war but by nuclear terrorism. Our governments understand that nuclear war can only result in the total destruction of the surface of the earth and death of the world's population. Unfortunately, terrorists don't care about the destruction of the earth or how many people they kill. What they care about is their religious beliefs and martyrdom. Unfortunately, religious terrorists are strongly motivated and are willing sacrifice their lives, without fear of death. That and enough money will provide them with whatever they need.

- **Dirty Bomb**: An explosive device that contains radioactive material but does not involve a nuclear explosion. The purpose of a Dirty Bomb is what is called area denial or preventing access to an area by making it radioactive.

- **Nuclear Winter**: This can be caused by the aftereffect of a nuclear war, but this can also be caused by extreme volcanic eruption or the impact of a meteorite. However caused, it is the result of particulate matter being trapped in the atmosphere for long periods of time. Blocking the suns radiation, killing most if not all of the plant and animal life, polluting all sources of water, the air we breathe, and eventually the population of the world through starvation and disease.

- **Electromagnetic Pulse**: Although created naturally by strong electromagnetic activity on the sun, an electromagnetic pulse or EMP can be created by man. Years ago man created the first EMP during the testing of nuclear weapons during the late 1940s and early 1950s. Although they were not as electronically dependent back then as we are today, they understood that the immediate effects of nuclear war would be the complete destruction of electronic communications across the globe.

- **IED, Improvised Explosive Device**: Anything can be used as a bomb, from a length of pipe to a pressure cooker. Any metal container can be used to make a bomb. Drop in a few pounds of explosives; add some nails, nuts and bolts, attach a detonator or a cell phone and that's it. It's not hard to build, which is the problem. The plans are on the internet, parts are easy to obtain, and explosives can be made in an average kitchen.

- **Chemical weapons**: Chemical weapons were first created during World War One as a way of killing or disabling large numbers of troops with man-made chemicals like mustard gas or cyanide gas. Today they can be created with instructions taken from the internet and some beans. Ricin, a toxic chemical that anyone can make, is a home spun terrorist favorite but often ineffectual tool. The panic that it can cause is real however, even if the substance is not pure and therefore not truly toxic.

- **Biological Weapons**: Simply put, man-made living organisms designed to kill. Biological Weapons of mass Destruction were outlawed by the 1972 Biological Weapons Convention. Unfortunately, countries that have created them are hesitant in destroying their stockpiles or divulging their ability manufacture them. Thus, the weapons remain a danger because without their destruction, they could fall, or be sold into the hands of a terrorist group.

Chapter Nine

How to react when disasters occur...

The most important first step to being a survivor of any disaster is to remain informed of the environment you live in and the world that surrounds you. While in some cases disasters occur without warning, most will give you at least a few minutes to a few hours of warning as long as you remain informed.

Chemical, Biological, Nuclear accidents or disaster:

☐ Once you have determined where the disaster has occurred, determine the prevailing wind direction that the chemical, nuclear, or biological agent may arrive from. If it's not probable that the effects will be approaching your home, then consider bugging in until the situation changes.

☐ If there is a threat of possible contamination but you have not been forced to evacuate, start by sealing your home with plastic sheeting and duct tape around your doors and windows, making your home as airtight as possible. If feasible, bring outdoor plants indoors to help remove carbon dioxide from your air supply.

☐ Gather what NBC *(Nuclear, Biological, and Chemical)* supplies you have, masks, Tyvek® Suits, Rubber boots, gloves and duct tape and explain to your family that they might be needed in the immediate future. Keep listening to your radio for updates and warnings. Once the evacuation order comes, don't be the last one out, be the first. Pre stage everything you plan on taking and get it stacked by the door.

☐ Once you evacuate, head diagonal to the prevailing wind. Most people will travel directly away from the contaminant source, but will follow the prevailing wind, gathering in large numbers in areas that eventually will be exposed.

Coronal Mass Discharge, Solar Flare, Electromagnetic Pulse:

☐ With adequate warning your electronics can be prepared to survive the damaging effects of an electromagnetic pulse. Unfortunately, once the damage has occurred, most electronics cannot be repaired, only replaced.

☐ First remove any and all batteries from the device. This includes any small button size batteries that may be attached to the main processor board. Once removed, the batteries should be stored separately from the device.

☐ Store electronic devices in layers of protection such as anti-static Mylar bags, metal containers, and even wrapped in alternating plastic bags and aluminum foil. This will allow EMP waves to flow around a device and not through it.

☐ Additionally, store your electronic devices in a Ferriday cage or something like an old refrigerator, microwave, or any type of well-grounded metal container.

Forest Fires:

☐ When you're told to evacuate, don't hesitate, just go. There are however, some steps you can take to help prevent the loss of your home when forest fires are approaching. The best protection is underground with a non-flammable barrier or door. Get yourself an underground pantry or shelter, and when your area comes under fire risk, start moving things underground.

☐ Cut back brush and trees a minimum 50 to 100 feet from your home. Angle the trees to fall away from your home and drag any brush as far back as you can.

☐ Turn your sprinklers on and if you can, put a sprinkler on the roof of your home. Get the area as wet as you can, even to the point of flooding your yard. Start early and leave it running until the water runs out or is cut off by the fire department.

☐ If you have a pool, get a gas powered pump or an electric powered pump that you can run off a generator should the power fail. You can even use a pressure washer as an emergency fire hose by just attaching water hoses to each end and dropping one end in a pool, pond, or lake and the other end to a sprinkler. Unfortunately, pressure washers have small gas tanks, but in an emergency, it might just save your home.

Extreme weather conditions, hurricanes and tornados:

☐ With both types of storms, your safest place would be indoors, in an interior room, preferably a bathroom with a deep metal tub and four solid walls. With a tornado, basements are safe as a bathroom just stick to the corners and away from windows or doors.

☐ If a hurricane is predicted to come your way, prepare your home by taping your windows or boarding them up. Pre-stage water supplies as your tap water might become tainted, filling bathtubs and other large water vessels. If you are living in an area that might be flooded, move things off the ground floor of your home or out of your basement.

☐ In hurricanes, basements are not suggested as they can be prone to flooding. After the storm has passed, check your home for damage or roof leaks and patch them as quickly as you can as follow up storms or additional bands of the same storm are the norm.

How you react to a disaster is just as important as how you prepare for disasters. Learn, be involved, be aware, be prepared and willing to do whatever it might take to ensure the survival of yourself and your family. The more you prepare, plan, and practice, the greater your chances of survival are.

Chapter Ten

Bug in prepping supplies, Zone One:

Prepping requirements are based on a single person, for a thirty day Bug In, and a minimum of a three day Bug Out. Individual requirements can vary depending on strength or health issues.

☐ A thirty day, minimum of 1200 calories of food per person, per day. Stock up on a variety and balanced mix of long term food supplies with a minimum shelf life of five years.

☐ A minimum of 12 ounces of water, for personal consumption, per person, per day. Additionally, your maximum water requirements can exceed one gallon, per person, per day. This includes water requirements for using toilets, personal hygiene, cooking, or cleaning.

☐ 30 days' worth of emergency lighting supplies. Calculate the number of GlowSticks®, flashlight batteries, candles, kerosene or lamp oil for lanterns, matches, and lighters you will need for between 4 to 12 hours of darkness per day. Also consider that any lighting in a darkened city may target you and your home. Keep thick blankets or cloth available to cover windows or doors.

☐ 30 days' worth of cooking equipment. However you plan on cooking or boiling water, ensure your supplies will last you through the duration of your Bug In. Candles can be used to boil water but are extremely inefficient, so consider purchasing a small, single burner gas grill for cooking or boiling water. Stock in enough fuel or gas to run your stove, once a day for thirty days. A charcoal grill or propane gas grill can be used during daylight hours but should never be used indoors.

☐ A small to medium gasoline or propane powered portable generator. Look for something in the 2000kw 3000kw peak kilowatt range. These generators will tend to be quieter and have longer lasting fuel tanks than larger models.

☐ 50 to 100 feet of grounded power cords and a surge strip.

☐ Between 10 and 15 gallons of gasoline that has been stabilized for long term storage. This should give you a thirty day supply of gas if burned at no more than half a gallon per day.

☐ Thirty gallons of chlorinated or purchased water in one gallon jugs or five gallon containers.

☐ Four to six cases of bottled water. 16oz bottles, 24 to 32 bottles per case.

☐ A water filtration device, funnel and pail.

☐ One hundred to two hundred feet of braided Polly rope with a test strength greater than your weight.

☐ At least two, 20 X 20, 8 mil thick plastic tarps

☐ Battery operated AM/FM/Weather radio.

☐ An empty backpack for each member of your family.

- [ ] A machete and large belt knife.

- [ ] A small axe or hatchet.

- [ ] A bundle of pre-seasoned fire wood.

- [ ] Matches, lighters, and fire starters.

- [ ] A roll or two of duct tape.

- [ ] Roll of black and red electrical tape.

- [ ] Multi tool with wire cutters and knife.

- [ ] A roll of 3 mill thick black plastic sheeting.

- [ ] A box of heavy duty construction grade trash bags.

- [ ] Simple first aid kit

- [ ] Self-defense items

Zone Two:

Prepping requirements are based on a single person, for a six month Bug In, and a minimum of a seven day Bug Out. Individual requirements can vary depending on strength or health issues.

- [ ] A minimum of 1200 calories of food per person, per day for six months. Stock up on a variety and balanced mix of long term, food supplies with a minimum shelf life of five to twenty years. Many providers of entrée based long term emergency food packaged multiple entrees in round or square containers, so check per meal calorie counts on the outside of each container. Plan on three to four meals per day if necessary to exceed the 1200 calorie minimum per day.

- [ ] A minimum of 12 ounces of potable water, for personal consumption, per person, per day. Additionally, your maximum water requirements can exceed one gallon, per person, per day so keep a minimum of thirty gallons on hand at all times for potable and gray water usage but the more you store, the longer you can hold out. Consider purchasing extra plastic trash cans with lids for water storage. Sizes can vary from thirty to fifty gallons but you will want to pre-measure the size of your showers and bathtubs for maximum storage. Store water in every shower but the one you are going to use for bathing. Remember that water stored in plastic trash cans may become tainted by the plastic you're storing it in, so only use it for gray water requirements like showers, toilets, cleaning or washing clothes. Potable water *(Drinking safe)* can only be stored in approved BPH free containers and only after being filtered or treated with a chlorinator.

- [ ] Store six months' worth of emergency lighting supplies. Calculate the number of candles, kerosene or lamp oil for hurricane lamps, GlowSticks®, flashlight batteries, matches and lighters, and Citronella oil used for Tiki torches you will need to provide adequate lighting for between 4 and 12 hours of darkness per day. Also consider that any lighting in a darkened city may target you and your home. Keep thick blankets or cloth available to cover windows or doors.

- ☐ Six months' worth of cooking equipment. Keep at least two full twenty pound tanks of propane on hand at all times if you plan on using your grill for cooking. Consider purchasing a small, single burner gas grill as a backup for cooking or boiling water. Stock in enough fuel or gas to run your stove once a day for thirty days should your main cooking device fail. *Never* use a charcoal grill or gas grill indoors and never at night.

- ☐ A small to medium gasoline or propane powered, portable generator. Look for something in the 4000kw to 6000kw range. These generators may hold between five and eight gallons of fuel and run for up to eight hours on a full tank of gas.

- ☐ 100 to 200 feet of grounded power cords and surge strips.

- ☐ Between 20 and 30 gallons of gasoline that has been stabilized for long term storage.

- ☐ Thirty to sixty gallons of chlorinated or distilled water.

- ☐ Six to ten cases of bottled water.

- ☐ A water filtration device, funnel and pail.

- ☐ One hundred to two hundred feet of braided Polly rope with a test strength greater than your weight.

- ☐ At least two, 20 X 20, 8 mil thick plastic tarps

- ☐ Battery operated AM/FM/Weather radio.

- ☐ An empty backpack for each member of your family.

- ☐ A machete and large belt knife.

- ☐ A chain saw and 6 bottles of oil/gasoline pre-mixed.

- ☐ A small axe or hatchet.

- ☐ A half to full cord of pre-seasoned fire wood.

- ☐ Matches, lighters, and fire starters.

- ☐ A roll or two of duct tape.

- ☐ Roll of black and red electrical tape.

- ☐ Multi tool with wire cutters and knife.

- ☐ A roll of 3 mill thick black plastic sheeting.

- ☐ A box of heavy duty construction grade trash bags.

- ☐ Simple first aid kit

- ☐ Self-defense items

Zone Three:

Prepping requirements are based on a single person, for a twelve months Bug In, and a minimum of a seven day Bug Out. Individual requirements can vary depending on strength or health issues.

- [ ] A minimum of 1200 calories of food per person, per day for twelve months. Stock up on a variety and balanced mix of long term food supplies with a minimum shelf life of five to twenty years. Many providers of entrée based long term emergency food packaged multiple entrees in round or square containers, so check per meal calorie counts on the outside of each container. Plan on three to four meals per day if necessary to exceed the 1200 calorie minimum per day.

- [ ] A minimum of 12 ounces of potable water, for personal consumption, per person, per day. Additionally, your maximum water requirements can exceed one gallon, per person, per day so keep a minimum of one hundred gallons on hand at all times for potable and gray water usage, but the more you store, the longer you can hold out. Consider purchasing extra plastic trash cans with lids for water storage. Sizes can vary from thirty to fifty gallons but you will want to pre-measure the size of your showers and bathtubs for maximum storage. Store water in every shower but the one you are going to use for bathing. Remember that water stored in plastic trash cans may become tainted by the plastic you're storing it in, so only use it for gray water requirements like showers, toilets, cleaning or washing clothes. Potable water *(Drinking safe)* can only be stored in approved BPH free containers and only after being filtered or treated with a chlorinator. Consider purchasing a stainless steel 55 gallon drum or food safe plastic water container.

- [ ] Store twelve months' worth of emergency lighting supplies. Calculate the number of candles, kerosene or lamp oil for hurricane lamps, GlowSticks, flashlight batteries, matches and lighters, or citronella oil used for tiki torches will be needed to provide some form of lighting for between 4 and 12 hours of darkness per day. Also consider that any lighting in a darkened city may target you and your home. Keep thick blankets or cloth available to cover windows or doors.

- [ ] Twelve months' worth of cooking equipment. Keep at least two full twenty pound tanks of propane on hand at all times if you plan on using your grill for cooking. Consider purchasing a small, single burner gas grill as a backup for cooking or boiling water. Stock in enough fuel or gas to run your stove, once a day for thirty days should your main cooking device fail. *Never* us a charcoal grill or gas grill indoors and never at night.

- [ ] A medium to large gasoline or propane powered portable generator in the 5000kw to 8000kw range. Additionally, try to obtain a unit that can be plugged into your home to supply power for everything essential within your home.

- [ ] 200 to 300 feet of grounded power cords and surge strips.

- [ ] Between 30 and 50 gallons of gasoline that has been stabilized for long term storage.

- [ ] One hundred gallons of chlorinated or distilled water.

- [ ] Ten to twelve cases of bottled water.

- ☐ A water filtration device, funnel and pail.
- ☐ One hundred to two hundred feet of braided Polly rope with a test strength greater than your weight.
- ☐ At least two, 20 X 20, 8 mil thick plastic tarps
- ☐ Battery operated AM/FM/Weather radio.
- ☐ An empty backpack for each member of your family.
- ☐ A machete and large belt knife.
- ☐ A chain saw and 6 bottles of a gas/oil pre-mixed.
- ☐ A large axe or maul.
- ☐ A full cord of pre-seasoned fire wood.
- ☐ Matches, lighters, and fire starters.
- ☐ Several rolls of duct tape.
- ☐ Roll of black and red electrical tape.
- ☐ Multi tool with wire cutters and knife.
- ☐ A roll of 3 mill thick black plastic sheeting.
- ☐ A box of heavy duty construction grade trash bags.
- ☐ A first aid kit.
- ☐ Self-defense items

Zone Four:

Senior Preppers need to consider putting on supplies for the long haul and for the possibility that other family members may show up at your door unannounced and without warning. Individual requirements can vary depending on strength or health issues.

- ☐ A minimum of 12 months or one years' worth of food per person. Stock up on a variety and balanced mix of long term, food supplies with a minimum shelf life of 10 to 20 years. Supplement it with pre consumer crops like wheat and corn. Plan on growing items you might normally buy at the store buy having heritage seeds to plant and plot a garden. Consider renewable farm animals like cattle, pigs, poultry, rabbits, and even goats. Re-learn skills like canning, dehydrating and or salting meats, baking bread from scratch and long term vegetable storage.

- ☐ A renewable and sustainable water supply. If you have a well, great, but have a hand pump available should your power supply fail. Find a way to store a minimum of 500 gallons in an above ground or below ground tank should your main water supply become tainted. Additionally, in your home keep a thirty day water supply, consisting of a minimum of 12 ounces of water, for personal consumption, per person, per day.

- Keep 12 months' worth of emergency lighting supplies on hand at all times. Calculate the number of GlowSticks®, flashlights, batteries, candles, kerosene or lamp oil for lanterns, matches and lighters you will need per night. Plan on burning as little as possible during the night. Having lighting when others don't makes you a target.

- 12 months' worth of cooking equipment. However you plan on cooking or boiling water, ensure your supplies will last you through the duration of your Bug In. Consider purchasing a small, single burner gas grill for cooking or boiling water. Stock in enough fuel, gas or wood to run your stove, once a day for a year. A charcoal grill, fire pit, or propane gas grill can be used during daylight hours but should never be used indoors.

- A folding survival blanket or poncho for each member of your family.

- A military grade First Aid Kit that includes a Surgical Kit with sutures and clamps. Breathing masks, latex or latex free gloves, and alcohol based hand sanitizer that can also be used as a fire starter.

- A large gasoline or propane powered, portable generator in the 5000kw to 8000kw range or a whole home generator designed to automatically start should your main supply of power fail. Additionally, consider alternative forms of power such as solar, wind or water sources that can remove your dependence completely from the grid.

- 200 to 300 feet of grounded power cords and surge strips.

- Between 200 and 500 gallons of stabilized gasoline or diesel fuel as needed for your generator, vehicles, and farm equipment.

- Ten to twelve cases of bottled water.

- A water filtration device, funnel and pail.

- One hundred to two hundred feet of braided Polly rope with a test strength greater than your weight.

- Chemical Gas masks and Tyvek painter's outfits.

- Rubber boots, heavy duty gloves and Safety goggles.

- Heavy duty tarps, hammer, nails and rope to tie them down.

- 3 mil thick plastic for sealing doors and windows.

- At least ten rolls of Duct tape and electrical tape.

- Heavy duty tools like an axe, sledge hammer, maul, or steel wedge for splitting wood.

- Complete Tool Kit for basic household or automotive repairs.

- Complete set of kitchen knives, folding pocket knives, sheath knives, machetes.

- Complete sewing kit, scissors, thread, needles.

- 250 feet of parachute cord, assorted colors.

- Length of bailing wire, barbed wire, fencing material.

- Spare batteries for vehicles and ATV's.

- Solar powered battery recharger
- Compact AM/FM/Weather Radio
- An empty backpack for each member of your family.
- A machete and large belt knife.
- A chain saw and 6 bottles of a gas/oil pre-mixed.
- A full cord or more of pre-seasoned fire wood.
- Matches, lighters, and fire starters.
- Multi tool with wire cutters and knife.
- A roll of 3 mill thick black plastic sheeting.
- A box of heavy duty construction grade trash bags.
- Self-defense items

Chapter Eleven

Bugging out, what stays and what goes…

When you think it's time to Bug Out, it's probably already too late. That's why preppers have pre staged Bug Out kits and bags. There are three types of pre staging; a vehicle survival kit, a three day bug out bag, and a seven day bug out bag.

Vehicle Survival Kit:

- ☐ A three day supply of food for each member of your family consisting of a minimum of 2000 calories of food per person, per day. Stick with long shelf life survival rations that can survive well in the heat of a vehicle.

- ☐ A three day supply of water for each member of your family, consisting of a minimum of 16 ounces of water, for personal consumption, per person, per day.

- ☐ Three days' worth of emergency lighting supplies. GlowSticks, flashlights and batteries, candles, plus matches and lighters. Get a small pot to boil water in, or a metal coffee can.

- ☐ Consider bringing some form of water filtration system, that way if you're stuck on the side of the road somewhere, you can filter any water you find, even the water in your radiator.

- ☐ A blanket, folding survival blanket, or poncho.

- ☐ A small bag of rock salt

- ☐ A folding shovel

- ☐ First Aid Kit, breathing masks, latex or latex free gloves, and alcohol based hand sanitizer that can also be used as a fire starter.

- ☐ A pocket multi tool.

- ☐ Small Tool kit containing screw drivers, pliers, wire cutters, a hammer.

- ☐ Tape: duct tape and electrical tape

- ☐ Jumper Cables or portable jump starter.

- ☐ Fifty feet of parachute cord

- ☐ Length of bailing wire

- ☐ Box of heavy duty, contractor grade trash bags.

- ☐ Cell phone battery recharger

- ☐ Compact AM/FM/Weather Radio

- ☐ Water Supplements that provide vitamins and essential electrolytes

- ☐ Permanent marker, writing pencil, pen and notepad.

- ☐ Toilet paper and sanitary wipes

Three Day Bug Out Bag

Each bug out bag should be designed for the family member who is going to carry it. Adult bags should carry most of the weight and food; children's bags should contain water and more of their personal items. Each bug out bag should be stocked with a minimum of three days' worth of food and water.

☐ A minimum of 2500 calories of food per person, per day for each adult, and a minimum of 1800 to 2000 kcals worth of food for children. Stock up on a variety and balanced mix of long term food supplies with a minimum shelf life of five years. Bring additional food supplies if your Bug Out requires walking long distances or climbing stairs.

☐ A minimum of 16 ounces of water, for personal consumption, per person, per day. Additionally, your maximum water requirements can exceed one gallon, per person, per day but as the weight of a gallon of water is 8.34 pounds. Three gallons of water weighs a little over 25 pounds and will fill up a backpack by itself. Consider bringing a form of water filtration system, allowing you to carry other emergency supplies instead of water weight.

☐ Three days' worth of emergency lighting supplies. GlowSticks, flashlights and batteries, candles, plus matches and lighters.

☐ Three days' worth of cooking equipment. Candles can be used to boil water but are extremely inefficient, so consider purchasing a small, single burner gas grill for cooking or boiling water. A small gas powered stove shouldn't use more than one tank of gas unless it's also used for providing heat. Purchase a small cooking pot for boiling water along with a camping mess kit that contains rugged silverware and a coffee cup.

☐ A folding survival blanket or poncho.

☐ First Aid Kit, breathing masks, latex or latex free gloves, and alcohol based hand sanitizer that can also be used as a fire starter.

☐ Personal hygiene items in travel kit form like a toothbrush, toothpaste, soap, shampoo, deodorant, dental floss, comb, and a washcloth or hand towel.

☐ A pocket tool or toolkit

☐ Folding pocket knife

☐ Pair of scissors

☐ Tape: duct tape and electrical

☐ Fifty feet of parachute cord

☐ Length of bailing wire

☐ Cell phone battery recharger

☐ Compact AM/FM/Weather Radio

☐ Water Supplements that provide vitamins and essential electrolytes

- [ ] Permanent marker, writing pencil, pen and notepad.
- [ ] Self-defense items

Seven day Bug Out Bag:

Each bug out bag should be designed for the family member who is going to carry it. Adult bags should carry most of the weight and food; children's bags should contain water and more of their personal items. Each bug out bag should be stocked with a minimum of seven days' worth of food and water.

- [ ] A minimum of 2500 calories of food per person, per day for each adult, and a minimum of 1800 to 2000 kcals worth of food for children. Stock up on a variety and balanced mix of long term food supplies with a minimum shelf life of five years. Bring additional food supplies if your Bug Out requires walking long distances or climbing stairs.

- [ ] A minimum of 16 ounces of water, for personal consumption, per person, per day. Additionally, your maximum water requirements can exceed one gallon, per person, per day but as the weight of a gallon of water is 8.34 pounds. Three gallons of water weighs a little over 25 pounds and will fill up a backpack by itself. Consider bringing a form of water filtration system, allowing you to carry other emergency supplies instead of water weight.

- [ ] Seven days' worth of emergency lighting supplies. GlowSticks, flashlights and batteries, candles, plus matches and lighters.

- [ ] Three days' worth of cooking equipment. Candles can be used to boil water but are extremely inefficient, so consider purchasing a small, single burner gas grill for cooking or boiling water. A small gas powered stove shouldn't use more than one tank of gas unless it's also used for providing heat. Purchase a small cooking pot for boiling water along with a camping mess kit that contains rugged silverware and a coffee cup.

- [ ] A folding survival blanket or poncho.

- [ ] First Aid Kit, breathing masks, latex or latex free gloves, and alcohol based hand sanitizer that can also be used as a fire starter.

- [ ] Personal hygiene items in travel kit form like a toothbrush, toothpaste, soap, shampoo, deodorant, dental floss, comb, and a washcloth or hand towel.

- [ ] A pocket tool or toolkit

- [ ] Folding pocket knife

- [ ] Pair of scissors

- [ ] Tape: duct tape and electrical

- [ ] Fifty feet of parachute cord

- [ ] Length of bailing wire

- [ ] Cell phone battery recharger

- [ ] Compact AM/FM/Weather Radio
- [ ] Water Supplements that provide vitamins and essential electrolytes
- [ ] Permanent marker, writing pencil, pen and notepad.
- [ ] Self-defense items

Chapter Twelve

Unarmed home defense...

First let me clarify that not everyone or every home has to have a gun in it. Firearms are a personal choice and if you chose not to have one, more power to you. I have steadfastly believed that home defense weapons are not limited to things that fire bullets. Anything, and I mean anything, can be used as a weapon. Your child's baseball bat, your husband's favorite golf club, that cheap bottle of wine you got as a gift for Christmas, an umbrella, cane, or just anything you have at hand. Deterrence is the first step in home security, and once you break the arm of an intruder, you can rest assured he will never try breaking into your home again.

My first suggestion in unarmed home defense is to purchase non-lethal devices like pepper spray and stun guns. Both can be purchased cheaply off the internet and can be stored near your entry points, out of sight, but not out of mind. Get a can of pepper spray and tape it to the top of your front door. High enough to be out of the reach of little fingers but close enough to be reached by adults should someone try and force their way through your front door. Next, get an umbrella stand and put it behind or adjacent to your front door. You can actually stock it with an umbrella or two but also throw in a little league baseball bat, heavy duty walking stick or cane, maybe even an axe handle, minus the axe. I would also suggest putting a door brace in it as anything that can be used to wedge between the door handle and the floor can also be used to smack someone upside the head.

Additionally, pre-position other self-defense weapons around your home in places you might find yourself in need. A baseball bat behind a bathroom door guarantees that if anyone chases you in there, well, they're not going to enjoy it after you're done with them. You can also take a small canister of pepper spray and tape it to the back of a bathroom door, and then, if they try pushing their way in, you can give them a face full.

Finally, if you're going to get a Taser or stun gun, learn how to properly use it and always keep it out of reach of children. Like your smoke alarm, the batteries of a stun gun or Taser should be checked every six months and recharged or changed out if needed.

Unarmed self-defense weapons can also include weapons that can kill but do not involve guns;

- ☐ Bows and arrows; re-curve, compound and crossbow.
- ☐ Martial arts weapons like nun chucks, swords, and throwing stars.
- ☐ Edged weapons; axes, hatchets, machetes, knives, swords, daggers or just a broken bottle will suffice.
- ☐ Chemical weapons like bleach, wasp and hornet spray (burns and disorients and will spray a long distance)
- ☐ Your bare hands. Always a last resort, never forget that your hands and feet are weapons too.

Chapter Thirteen

Armed home defense...

Armed self-defense is a life choice, one that no one can make for you but you have to make yourself. Becoming a gun owner, you have to understanding and accept that with the ownership of a gun comes the possibility you may have to use it to take the life of another. With the ownership of a weapon comes the responsibility of getting the proper training and learning the proper safety and storage a weapon requires. First, check your local city, county and state laws on the requirements for the legal ownership of a handgun or rifle.

Using the state of Georgia for an example:

In the state of Georgia, to purchase a new handgun, rifle, or shotgun from a registered FFL (Federal Firearm License) dealer, you are required to fill out an Over-the-Counter, Firearms Transaction Record, Form 4473.

Handgun ownership in the state of Georgia does not require a concealed weapons permit unless you plan on carrying your handgun concealed. Georgia does require proof of residency in the form of a Georgia driver's license and requires the purchaser be at least 18 years of age. There is no waiting period for purchasing handguns in Georgia and convicted felons are not allowed to purchase handguns.

In Georgia, rifle and shotgun purchases do not require Georgia residency but do require proper ID in the form of a driver's license or passport and that you be of at least 18 years of age. Residents from other states may travel across state lines to make purchases. Again, there is no waiting period for purchasing rifles and shotguns in Georgia, and convicted felons are not allowed to buy them. Private sales or estate sales are allowed in the state of Georgia without a federal background check and do not require re-registration or transfer of ownership.

Other Considerations...

First, understand what type of weapons you will need for the types of environments you live in. Each home should contain a minimum of one handgun and one rifle per member of your family. Weapon sizes and calibers are only limited to the ability of each family member so consider taking your family to an indoor range where you can rent different size weapons and test what your family members are most comfortable with.

The average soldier carries between 300 and 500 rounds of pistol and rifle ammunition at any given time. For a civilian, Bug Out or patrolling expectations should not exceed common sense. For handguns, consider carrying approximately 50 rounds in preloaded magazines. For automatic rifles or camp rifles you should carry around six, thirty-round magazines at any given time. At your home, your stockpile of ammunition should be calculated by the number of weapons you have per caliber, times the minimum amount of ammunition you should stockpile for each weapon. For revolvers, shotguns and bolt action rifles, calculate a minimum of 200 rounds per weapon. For semi-automatic handguns and rifles, calculate a minimum of 500 rounds per weapon. For example; if you have two adults that are each comfortable carrying a semi-automatic 9 mm handgun and a AR-15 style .223 caliber rifle, then you should keep a minimum of 1,000 rounds of both 9 mm and .223 ammo stockpiled at all times.

For children, start them training on .22LR caliber weapons and handguns. Ironically, .22lr ammunition is the lowest cost ammunition, but one of the few ammunitions that can't be reloaded. This fact makes it ideal as training ammunition and as harassment ammunition as well. Think of it as a noisy cricket, something that would be hard pressed to hit a target at distances further then 50 yards, but it will help to keep someone's head down, make their aim shaky and inaccurate, and allow adult shooters the ability to be more accurate, have more time on target, and waste less costly ammunition. Think of it this way, calculating cost, for every one round fired through a .30-06 rifle, you can shoot 30 or 40 rounds through a .22lr. Stockpiles of .22lr ammunition should be in excess of 2,000 rounds per weapon as it is a cost effective training aid, and barter supply.

Armed self-defense weapons can also include:

- ☐ Bows and arrows; re-curve, compound and crossbow.
- ☐ Martial arts weapons like nun chucks, swords, and throwing stars.
- ☐ Edged weapons; axes, hatchets, machetes, knives, swords, daggers or just a broken bottle will suffice.
- ☐ Chemical weapons like bleach, acid, wasp and hornet spray.
- ☐ Your bare hands. Always a last resort, never forget that your hands and feet are weapons too.

Chapter Fourteen

Rings of protection...

Once a disaster occurs, and the government fails, when law enforcement starts worrying more about their own families than yours, and your safety and security becomes your own responsibility, you're going to have to take the steps necessary to defend yourself or be willing to evacuate to some place you can feel safe. Once you have your floor plan and the layout of your property you need to break it down into Five Rings and determine what weapons you will need to defend each zone.

Ring Five: Defined as the area from your property line to as far as you can see or be seen. Take into account your shooting abilities when looking at this distance because if you were once a Marine Corps Sniper, then shooting out to 500 or 1,000 yards might be second nature. For most of us however, a more attainable distance would be between 100 and 300 yards. Even at this distance your weapon of choice should be something in a high caliber, bolt action or semi-automatic rifle, with a sling and a powerful scope. This may not be your primary defensive weapon but where ever you store it, store at least 100 rounds of ammunition at all times. If your shots are on the mark, you won't need a lot of this ammo. Warning shots will deter most intruders, and if not, just wait until they get closer and your accuracy will improve.

Ring Four: Defined as the area inside your property line to the outside of your house. Depending on the size of your property, this area could be as small as 500 square feet to 500 square acres. In reality, distances are more likely to be limited to your line of sight, but your weapon of choice can vary from something in a high caliber, bolt action or semi-automatic rifle, to a 12 gauge automatic or pump action shotgun. You also need to consider outside landscaping, storage buildings and other yard obstacles that people can hide behind. Finally, consider how you're going to aim. Iron sights are great if your target is within sight range but a red dot or laser assisted scope increases your chances of hitting your target faster and with less wasted ammunition.

Ring Three: This area is tightly defined as the entry points of your home. This includes doors, windows, garage doors, walls or weak spots in your home's exterior. Defending this area, you're going to want something with projectile mass, projectile numbers, and with a semi rapid rate of fire. My first suggestion would be any caliber of pump or automatic shotgun but not anything in a single barrel, or double barrel. Add a pistol grip, an 8 round tube magazine loaded with home defense, 00 buck, single 0, number 1 through 4 shot. Personal defensive loads are also available for the .410 caliber shotgun that contains a mixture of copper jacketed slugs and steel shot. turkey loads or rifled slugs. Shotguns are highly effective, extremely low maintenance and deliver impact without accuracy therefore making them a great choice for Ring three defense. The idea here is to react quickly and stop any intruder from entering the perimeter of your home. Second choice would be something in a semi-automatic carbine class. Carbines come in many types, such as leaver action, pump or semi-automatic. Calibers sizes vary from as small as .22Lr up to .40 and .45. Personally it is my belief that the size of the bullet doesn't matter, just how much lead you can put into a target.

Ring Two: This area is defined as the outside rooms of your home, those rooms where at least one wall of the room is part of the outside of your home. In these areas your choice of weapons can vary from as heavy a caliber as a shotgun to semi-automatic rifles and handguns. On your floor plan mark these points as your primary stand your ground points of defense.

Ring one: This is a loosely defined Ring that covers most interior rooms of your home including all rooms that don't have one wall touching the outside of your home, and are fall back points or second points of defense. These points will need to be someplace where you can safely store secondary personal weapons of choice. For those of you who still consider non-lethal force an option, think about items that will stop a person in their tracks. Knives, pepper-spray on a shelf, Tasers, stun guns, etc., just make sure it is any weapon that can be close at hand and out of the reach of children.

Zone Zero: This is your final defense point, your safe room, and your last stand. First you need to pick out and designate a panic/safe room. It needs to be on the first floor of your home or in a basement. Find a first floor room with an outside wall but no windows, or an inner bathroom with a metal bathtub and no windows. In a basement, find a corner room with at least two walls that are solid concrete or concrete block. Now check the door to your panic room. Is it solid core or a hollow core door? Does it contain a simple latch lock or something solid? Consider replacing it with a steel reinforced door or even consider replacing it with a hardwood or metal door. Can your door lock be replaced or a dead bolt added? Consider ways that your door can be reinforced with latches, locks and braces that will prevent or deter a criminal from gaining access to your panic room, even simple things like a wedge of wood that can be forced under the door to help prevent someone from opening it..

Put a small to medium safe in the corner of your panic room and disguise it as a small table, either with a tablecloth, or, if you are crafty, build a small table that the safe will fit under. Add to it the following: two handguns - one revolver, one automatic, 50 rounds of ammo for each and a brand new, un-opened disposable cell phone. Pick handguns that are low in caliber, .22LR, .25 auto, .32 auto, and .380. Something that anyone, be it your wife or children can load, chamber and fire. Stock some ear plugs and goggles for safety and shooting in closed spaces. Additionally, if your panic room is a bathroom put the following under the sink; a supply of water, granola or meal replacement bars, a flashlight, extra batteries, a very sharp knife, axe or hatchet, and a fire extinguisher. If your panic room is a closet, add a five gallon bucket, toilet paper, and some trash bags to use for a toilet.

Now introduce your family to your panic room, show them the quickest routes to get there and how to lock things down. Teach them to get in the room, lock the door, lie down in the bathtub, and call 911. Show your family how to respect, use, and shoot your guns. Involve them in their own protection. Tell them about your home defenses, let them make the choice to be involved or not and respect their decision.

Chapter Fifteen

Why I'm a Prepper...

I can't think of a better way to say this, but prepping isn't something you're going to learn from one book, or even ten. It's something that you can only learn with time, effort, and practice. I've been a Prepper and survivalist for over thirty years now starting as a Boy Scout, then as a member of the Civil Air Patrol, before joining the military. By the time I turned twenty I realized that being prepared for any disaster, man-made or act of nature was not only smart but a necessary skill set if I wanted to survive.

In Florida I lived through hurricanes. In California I learned how the earth moves by surviving the Northridge Earthquake. In Illinois I learned how the sound of a tornado *does* resemble a freight train, and in South Dakota I experienced a blizzard of 56 inches of snow and a wind chill of minus eighty degrees. From it all I learned to respect weather and to *never* underestimate the destruction it can cause.

I put plans into action after 9/11 and again after Hurricane Katriana which affected the flow of gasoline, power and supplies to the area in which I live. Neither of those events forced me to go into long term survival mode, but I was prepared to do so, which was the point.

Then I chose a career in law enforcement and from it I learned how to defend myself from others, how to react in an emergency, and how to help others in need. I also learned that I didn't like being shot at and that at the time; law enforcement was more political than it was about enforcing the laws. Today, Law Enforcement and police officers are well trained, well respected and willing to enforce the laws that they are entrusted with.

After law enforcement I was teetering back and forth between becoming a survivalist or a prepper so I studied them both. A survivalist goes out in the woods, builds fires by rubbing sticks together, eats grubs and drinks snow that *isn't* yellow, and sleeps in a tent out in the cold. Preppers use a lighter or matches to start a fire, eats emergency food or survival rations, drinks water that has been filtered or bottled, and if they have to sleep in a tent it usually involves a queen size air mattress, sleeping bags and pillows.

So I became a Prepper...

To me, Prepping is more than just learning, *which never ends,* it's a willingness to teach others how to prep and survive disasters. Those who want to be Preppers need to understand that there may come a time where the government, or those in political power, may be unable, unwilling, or slow to respond in a disaster, and you and your family's survival will be in your hands alone.

APPENDICES

Appendix A – Food Storage Guidelines For Consumers*

348-960 (FST-66P)

Renee Boyer, Extension specialist, Food Science and Technology, Virginia Tech; Julie McKinney, Project Associate, Food Science and Technology, Virginia Tech

Purchase Fresh Food

Provide safe and nutritious food for you and your family by purchasing food within the food manufacturer's freshness dates. Meat, fish, poultry, dairy, and fresh bakery products are dated with a "sell by date" to indicate how long the food can be displayed for sale. Also, the "sell by date" allows a reasonable amount of time after the purchase in which the product can be used. Consumers should always purchase food before the "sell by date" expires. Cereals, snack foods, frozen entrees, and dry packaged foods may be marked with a "best if used by date." The products are not at their best quality after this date, but can still be used safely for a short period of time thereafter. Other foods, such as unbaked breads, are marked with an "expiration" or "use by date," which means the product should not be consumed after that date. Do not purchase any food not used by that date. The freshness date is located on the food package and serves as an indicator of product quality.

Some foods, such as canned foods, have a product code stamped on the bottom or top of each container providing information such as "use by date" or "best quality date," the name of the plant where the food was manufactured, and the lot number. The code number may not be consistent from one manufacturer to another. For instance, food manufacturers may indicate the "use by date" as month and year (APR02) stamped on top of the can. APR02 means the food should be consumed by April of 2002. The first letter and number (corresponding to month and year) of the stamped code also may indicate "use by dates." F2 would indicate that the product is of highest quality if consumed by June of 2002. Consumers may contact the food manufacturer directly to determine "use by dates." Many food manufacturers provide a 1-800 number for consumer questions. Generally, canned goods have a one-year expiration date from the date of manufacture before quality diminishes.

When grocery shopping, pick-up refrigerated and frozen foods just prior to checkout. Refrigerated foods should be cold, and frozen foods should be solid with no evidence of thawing. Refrigerated and frozen food should be bagged together. After grocery shopping, drive straight home and store food in the refrigerator or freezer. It is important to keep refrigerated and frozen foods out of the danger zone of 40°F to 140°F.

Proper Storage Extends Shelf-Life of Food

The shelf-life of food will depend upon the food itself, packaging, temperature, and humidity. If the food is not sterilized, it will ultimately spoil due to the growth of microorganisms. Foods, such as dairy products, meats, poultry, eggs, and fresh fruits and vegetables, will spoil rapidly if not stored at proper temperatures. For optimal quality and safety, dairy products should be stored at refrigerated temperatures between 34°F and 38°F, meats between 33°F and 36°F, and eggs 33°F to 37°F. Fresh vegetables and ripe fresh fruits should be stored between 35°F and 40°F. Always store refrigerated foods at temperatures less than 40°F. Place a thermometer in the refrigerator and monitor the temperature often. This is especially important during the hot summer months.

Frozen foods should be stored below 0°F in moisture-proof, gas-impermeable plastic or freezer wrap. Make sure to label and date frozen foods. Frozen foods may be safe to eat if stored beyond the recommended storage time but quality may diminish. Sometimes consumers will overload a freezer and block the circulation of coolant throughout the freezer compartment. This will lower the efficiency of the freezer in keeping the food below 0°F.

Food that is temperature abused will spoil rapidly as evidenced by off-odors, off-flavors, off-color, and/or soft texture. For instance, spoiled milk exhibits a fruity off-odor, acid taste, and may curdle, whereas spoilage of fresh fruits and vegetables may exhibit an off-color and soft texture. Slime on the surface of meat, poultry, and fish indicates spoilage. As microorganisms grow, they utilize the food as a nutrient source and may produce acids. There is an increased risk of food-borne illness from consumption of spoiled food. Food may be spoiled without a detectable off-odor. **Discard all foods that may have been at room temperature more than 2 hours. Therefore, when in doubt throw it out!**

To ensure food stored in the refrigerator, freezer, or pantry is consumed within the expiration dates, practice **FIFO (First-In-First-Out)**. When stocking food storage areas, place recently purchased items behind the existing food items. This will help ensure that you are consuming food prior to expiration date/spoilage and will save you money by reducing the amount of food to discard. Portion leftovers in clean, sanitized, shallow containers, and cover, label, and date. Generally, leftovers should be discarded after 48 hours in the refrigerator.

Dry food staples such as flour, crackers, cake mixes, seasonings, and canned goods should be stored in their original packages or tightly closed airtight containers below 85°F (optimum 50°F to 70°F). Humidity levels greater than 60% may cause dry foods to draw moisture, resulting in caked and staled products. Canned goods stored in high humidity areas may ultimately rust, resulting in leaky cans. Discard canned goods that are swollen, badly dented, rusted, and/or leaking.

For safety, always store food separate from nonfood items such as paper products, household cleaners, and insecticides. Contamination of food or eating utensils with a household cleaner or insecticide could result in a chemical poisoning.

What To Do When The Power Goes Out

When the power goes out in the home, minimize opening the refrigerator and freezer. Refrigerators and freezers are insulated, aiding in keeping foods cold. However, if the refrigerator or freezer door is opened often, the cooling will be lost. Perishable refrigerated foods (i.e. foods of animal origin) should be discarded after a 6-hour period. Using block ice may increase shelf-life of refrigerated foods. Food stored in fully loaded freezers may last for approximately two days, whereas food stored in partially loaded freezers may last for only one day. Freezer foods may be refrozen if ice crystals are present. Exceptions include ice cream, pizza, and casseroles. If the frozen food has completely thawed but is cold, it must be cooked within a 24-hour period; or foods may be refrozen within 24 hours after thawing. However, quality may be diminished. If in doubt about when the food actually thawed in the freezer, discard the thawed food. Dry ice may be used to keep frozen foods frozen and cold foods cold. Be careful not to handle dry ice with bare hands or breathe the vapors.

Recommended Storage For Various Foods

Breads, Cereals, Flour and Rice

Bread should be stored in the original package at room temperature and used within 5 to 7 days. However, bread stored in the refrigerator will have a longer shelf-life due to delayed mold growth and may be firmer. Expect a 2- to 3-month shelf-life of bread stored in the freezer. Refrigerate *cream style bakery goods* containing eggs, cream cheese, whipped cream and/or custards no longer than 3 days.

Cereals may be stored at room temperature in tightly closed containers to keep out moisture and insects. *Whole wheat flour* may be stored in the refrigerator or freezer to retard rancidity of the natural oils.

Store *raw white rice* in tightly closed containers at room temperature and use within one year. *Brown* and *wild rice* stored at room temperature will have a shorter shelf-life (6 months) due to the oil becoming rancid. Shelf-life of raw white and brown rice may be extended by refrigeration. *Cooked rice* may be stored in the refrigerator for 6 to 7 days or in the freezer for 6 months.

Fresh Vegetables

Removing air (oxygen) from the package, storing the vegetables at 40°F refrigerated temperatures, and maintaining optimum humidity (95 to 100%) may extend shelf-life of fresh vegetables. Most fresh vegetables may be stored up to 5 days in the refrigerator. Always wrap or cover fresh leafy vegetables in moisture-proof bags to retain product moisture and prevent wilting. *Root vegetables* (potatoes, sweet potatoes, onions, etc.) and *squashes, eggplant*, and *rutabagas* should be stored in a cool, well-ventilated place between 50°F and 60°F. *Tomatoes* continue to ripen after harvesting and should be stored at room temperature. Removing the tops of *carrots, radishes,* and *beets* prior to refrigerator storage will reduce loss of moisture and extend shelf-life. Palatability of *corn* diminishes during cold storage due to elevated starch content. *Corn* and *peas* should be stored in a ventilated container. *Lettuce* should be rinsed under cold running water, drained, packaged in plastic bags, and refrigerated. Proper storage of fresh vegetables will maintain quality and nutritive value.

Processed Vegetables

Canned vegetables can be stored in a cool, dry area below 85°F (optimum 50°F to 70°F) for up to one year. After one year, canned vegetables may still be consumed. However, overall quality and nutritional value may have diminished. Discard badly dented, swollen, and/or rusty cans.

Frozen vegetables may be stored in the freezer for 8 months at 0°F. *Dehydrated vegetables* should be stored in a cool, dry place and used within 6 months since they have a tendency to lose flavor and color. *Home prepared vegetables* should be blanched prior to freezing. For more information on home food preservation see VCE Publication 348-576, Freezing Fruits & Vegetables (http://pubs.ext.vt.edu/348-596/).

Fresh Fruit

In general, store fresh fruit in the refrigerator or in a cold area to extend shelf-life. Reduce loss of moisture from fresh fruit by using, covered containers. Always store fresh fruit in a separate storage area in the refrigerator, since fresh fruits may contaminate or absorb odors from other foods. **Prior to consumption, rinse fresh fruits and vegetables under cold running water to remove possible pesticide residues, soil, and/or bacteria.** Peeling, followed by washing of fresh fruits and vegetables, is also very efficient in removing residues.

Ripe eating *apples* should be stored separately from other foods in the refrigerator and eaten within one month. Apples stored at room temperature will soften rapidly within a few days. Remember to remove apples that are bruised or decayed prior to storage in the refrigerator. Do not wash apples prior to storage.

Green pears and *apricots* should be ripened at room temperature and then stored in the refrigerator. Expect a 5-day refrigerated shelf-life for these fruits.

Unripe *peaches* may be ripened at room temperature and eaten after 2 days. Store ripe peaches in the refrigerator but consume at room temperature.

Grapes and *plums* should be stored in the refrigerator and eaten fresh within 5 days of purchase. Store unwashed grapes separately from other foods in the refrigerator and wash prior to consumption.

Ripe *strawberries* can be stored in the refrigerator separately from other foods for approximately 3 days. Strawberries should be washed and stemmed prior to consumption.

Citrus fruits, such as lemons, limes, and ripened oranges, can be stored in the refrigerator for 2 weeks. Grapefruit may be stored at a slightly higher temperature of 50°F.

Melons, such as the honeydew melon, cantaloupe, and watermelon, may be ripened at room temperature for 2, 3, and 7 days, respectively. Store ripe melons in the refrigerator.

Avocados and *bananas* should be ripened at room temperature for 3 to 5 days. Never store unripe bananas in the refrigerator, since cold temperatures will cause the bananas to rapidly darken.

Processed Fruit

Canned fruit and *fruit juices* may be stored in a cool, dry place below 85°F (optimum 50°F to 70°F) for one year. As with canned vegetables, badly dented, bulging, rusty, or leaky cans should be discarded. *Dried fruits* have a long shelf-life because moisture has been removed from the product. Unopened dried fruits may be stored for 6 months at room temperature.

Dairy Products

The shelf-life of *fluid milk* stored in the refrigerator (<40°F) will range from 8 to 20 days depending upon the date of manufacture and storage conditions in the grocers' shelf. Milk is a very nutritious and highly perishable food. Milk should never be left at room temperature and always capped or closed during refrigerator storage. Freezing milk is not recommended, since the thawed milk easily separates and is susceptible to development of off-flavors.

Dry milk may be stored at cool temperatures (50°F to 60°F) in airtight containers for one year. Opened containers of dry milk, especially whole milk products, should be stored at cold temperatures to reduce off-flavors. Handle reconstituted milk like fluid milk and store at refrigeration temperatures if not immediately used.

Canned evaporated milk and *sweetened condensed milk* may be stored at room temperature for 12 to 23 months. Refrigerate opened canned milk and consume within 8 to 20 days.

Natural and *processed cheese* should be kept tightly packaged in moisture-resistant wrappers and stored below 40°F. Surface mold growth on hard natural cheese may be removed with a clean knife and discarded. Rewrap cheese to prevent moisture loss. Presence of mold growth in processed cheese, semi-soft cheese, and cottage cheese is an indicator of spoilage and thus these foods should be discarded.

Store commercial *ice cream* at temperatures below 0°F. Expected shelf-life of commercial ice cream is approximately 2 months before quality diminishes. Immediately return opened ice cream to the freezer to prevent loss of moisture and development of ice crystals. Store ice cream at constant freezer temperatures to slow growth of ice crystals.

Meats, Poultry, Fish, and Eggs

Meat, poultry, fish, and *eggs* are highly perishable and potentially hazardous due to their high moisture and high protein content. Generally, *fresh cuts* of meat contain spoilage bacteria on the surface that will grow, produce slime, and cause spoilage after 3 days of refrigerator storage in oxygen-permeable packaging film. *Ground meat products* are more susceptible to spoilage due to the manufacturing process and increased surface area of the product. Bacteria in ground meats are distributed throughout, providing rapid growth in the presence of air. Ground meats should be stored on the lower shelf of the refrigerator and used within 24 hours of purchase. Refrigerator storage slows bacterial growth; however, the product will eventually spoil. Optimum storage temperature of refrigerated meats, including ground beef, is 33°F to 36°F.

Freezing inhibits the growth of bacteria. Whole cuts of meat may be stored in the freezer ranging from 4 to 12 months, whereas ground meat may be stored for 3 to 4 months. For maximum storage, wrap meats in moisture-proof, gas impermeable packaging to prevent freezer burn.

Cured meats, such as bacon, should be stored in their original packaging in the refrigerator. Cured meats have a tendency to become rancid when exposed to air. Therefore, rewrap cured meats after opening the package. Expect approximately a 1-week shelf-life for cured meats. Vacuum-packaging (absence of air) and modified atmospheric packaging (partial removal of air) extends shelf-life of meats and meat products (i.e. luncheon meats). The shelf-life of vacuum-packaged meats and gas-flushed meats is 14 days and 7 to 12 days, respectively.

Poultry should be prepared within 24 hours of purchase or stored in the freezer. Poultry may be stored in the freezer (0°F) for 12 months. **Thaw poultry in the refrigerator, under cold running water, or in the microwave. Cook poultry parts (i.e. breast and roast) and whole poultry to an internal temperature of 170°F, and 180°F, respectively.** Leftovers stored in the refrigerator should be consumed within 3 days and reheated to 165°F prior to consumption. Poultry broth and gravy should not be stored more than 2 days in the refrigerator and reheated to a full boil (212°F) before consuming.

Fresh *fish*, *shrimp*, and *crab* stored in the refrigerator (slightly above 32°F) should be consumed within 1 to 2 days. Never store fresh fish in water due to leaching of nutrients, flavor, and pigments. Frozen fresh lean fish and seafood (except shrimp) may be stored for 3 to 6 months at 0°F. Shrimp may be stored for 12 months at 0°F.

Eggs should be purchased refrigerated and stored in the refrigerator (33°F to 37°F) in their original carton. Storage of eggs in the original carton reduces absorption of odors and flavors from other foods stored in the refrigerator. Use eggs within 3 to 5 weeks of the "pack date" listed on the carton (1 to 365 representing pack date day within the year). Leftover egg yolks and egg whites may be stored in the refrigerator covered for 2 and 4 days, respectively. Cover egg yolks with water. *Hard-boiled eggs* may be stored in the refrigerator for 1 week, whereas *pasteurized liquid eggs* may be stored in the refrigerator for 10 days. Egg whites and pasteurized eggs may be stored at freezer temperatures for one year. *Shell eggs* should never be stored in the freezer. *Dried eggs* may be stored in tightly closed containers in the refrigerator for one year.

Water

Commercial bottled water has an extended shelf-life of one to two years due to extensive water treatment (filtration, demineralization, and ozonation) and strict environmental controls during manufacturing and packaging. Bottled water should be stored in a cool, dry place in the absence of sunlight. Household tap water has a limited shelf-life of only a few days due to the growth of microorganisms during storage. Therefore, consumers should purchase bottled water if planning to store water for extended periods. The Food and Drug Administration (FDA) regulates commercial bottled water as a food. For more information on bottled water see VCE publication 356-486, Buying Bottled Water (http://pubs.ext.vt.edu/356-486/).

Recommended Food Storage Chart

The following charts provide general recommended storage times from date of purchase for various food products stored under optimum conditions. Storage generally is not recommended under conditions where no time is listed in the chart. For maximum shelf-life, consumers should always purchase fresh food and never temperature abuse food. If a product has a "use-by" date, follow that date. If a product has a "sell-by" date or no date, cook or freeze the product within the times indicated on this chart.

Food	Pantry (Room Temperature)	Refrigerator (33°F to 40°F)	Freezer (0°F)
Bread and Cereal Products			
Baked quick breads	4-5 days	1-2 weeks	2-3 months
Bread	5-7 days	1-2 weeks	3 months
Bread crumbs and croutons	6 months		
Bread rolls, unbaked		2-3 weeks	1 month
Cereals, ready-to-eat	1 year 2-3 months*		
Cereals, ready-to-cook	6 months		
Corn meal	1 year	18 months	2 years
Doughnuts	4-5 days		3 months
Flour, all-purpose, white	6-8 months	1 year	1-2 years
Flour, whole wheat		6-8 months	1-2 years
Pasta	2 years		
Pies and pastries		3 days	4-6 months
Pies and pastries, baked			1-2 months
Pies and pastries, cream filled		2-3 days	3 months
Pizza		3-4 days	1-2 months
Rice, brown	6 months		

Rice, white	1 year	6-7 days[+]	6 months[+]
Tacos, enchiladas, and burritos (frozen)		2 weeks	1 year
Waffles		4-5 days	1 month
Packaged Foods and Mixes			
Biscuit, brownie, and muffin mixes	9 months		
Cakes, prepared	2-4 days		2-3 months
Cake mixes	6-9 months		
Casserole mix	9-12 months		
Chili powder	6 months		
Cookies, packaged	2 months		8-12 months
Crackers, pretzels	3 months		
Frosting, canned	3 months		
Frosting, mix	8 months		
Fruit cake		2-3 months	1 year
Hot roll mix	18 months		
Instant breakfast products	6 months		
Pancake and piecrust mix	6 months		
Pancake waffle batter		1-2 days	3 months
Toaster pastries	3 months		
Sauce and gravy mixes	6 months		
Soup mixes	1 year		
Spices, Herbs, Condiments, Extracts			
Catsup, chili, and cocktail sauce	1 year 1 month*	6 months	
Herbs	6 months		1-2 years

Herb/spice blends	2 years 1 year *		1-2 years
Mustard	2 years	6-8 months*	8-12 months
Spices, ground	6 months		1-2 years
Spices, whole	1-2 years		2-3 years
Vanilla extract	2 years 1 year*		
Other extracts	1 year		
Other Food Staples			
Bacon bits	4 months		
Baking powder	18 months		
Baking soda	2 years		
Bouillon products	1 year		
Carbonated soft drinks (12 oz. cans)	6-9 months		
Carbonated soft drinks, diet (12 oz. cans)	3-4 months		
Chocolate, premelted	1 year		
Chocolate syrup	2 years	6 months*	
Chocolate, semisweet	2 years		
Chocolate, unsweetened	18 months		
Cocoa mixes	8 months		
Coconut, shredded	1 year 6 months*	8 months	1 year
Coffee cans	2 years 2 weeks*	2 months	6 months
Coffee, instant	6 months 2 weeks*		
Coffee, vacuum-packed	1 year ^		

103

Coffee lighteners (dry)	9 months 6 months*		1 year
Cornstarch	18 months		2 years
Gelatin	18 months		
Honey, jams, jellies, and syrup	1 year	6-8 months*	
Marshmallows	2-3 months		
Marshmallow cream	3-4 months		
Mayonnaise	2-3 months	12 months 2 months*	
Molasses	2 years		
Nuts, shelled	4 months	6 months	
Nuts, unshelled	6 months		
Nuts, salted			6-8 months
Nuts, unsalted			9-12 months
Oil, salad	3 months^ 2 months*		
Parmesan grated cheese	10 months 2 months*		
Pasteurized process cheese spread	3 months	3-4 weeks*	4 months
Peanut butter	6-9 months 2-3 months*	4-6 months	
Popcorn	1-2 years	2 years	2-3 years
Pectin	1 year		
Salad dressings, bottled	1 year^	3 months*	
Soft drinks	3 months		
Artificial sweetener	2 years		
Sugar, brown	4 months		

Sugar, confectioners	18 months		
Sugar, granulated	2 years		
Tea bags	18 months		
Tea, instant	2 years		
Vegetable oils	6 months 1-3 months*		
Vegetable shortening	3 months	6-9 months	
Vinegar	2 years 1 year*		
Water, bottled	1-2 years		
Whipped topping (dry)	1 year		
Yeast, dry	Pkg. exp. date		

Vegetables

Asparagus		2-3 days	8 months
Beets		2 weeks	
Broccoli		3-5 days	
Brussels sprouts		3-5 days	
Cabbage		1 week	
Carrots		2 weeks	
Cauliflower		1 week	
Celery		1 week	
Corn (husks)		1-2 days	8 months
Cucumbers		1 week	
Eggplant		1 week	
Green beans		1-2 days	8 months
Green peas		3-5 days	8 months

Lettuce		1 week	
Lima beans		3-5 days	8 months
Mushrooms		2 days	
Onions	1 week	3-5 days	
Onion rings (precooked, frozen)			1 year#
Peppers		1 week	
Pickles, canned	1 year	1 month*	
Frozen potatoes			8 month
Sweet potatoes	2-3 weeks		
White potatoes	2-3 months		
Potato chips	1 month		
Radishes		2 weeks	
Rhubarb		3-5 days	
Rutabagas	1 week		
Snap beans		1 week	
Spinach		5-7 days	8 months
Squash, Summer		3-5 days	
Squash, Winter	1 week		
Tomatoes		1 week	
Turnips		2 weeks	
Commercial baby food, jars	1-2 years^	2-3 days	
Canned vegetables	1 year^	3-5 days*	
Canned vegetables, pickled	1 year^	1-2 months*	
Dried vegetables	6 months		
Frozen vegetables			8 months

Vegetable soup		3-4 days	3 months
Fruits			
Apples	Until ripe	1 month	
Apricots	Until ripe	5 days	
Avocados	Until ripe	5 days	
Bananas	Until ripe	5 days (fully ripe)	
Berries	Until ripe	3 days	1 year
Canned fruit	1 year	2-4 days*	
Canned fruit juices	1 year	3-4 days*	
Cherries	Until ripe	3 days	
Citrus fruit	Until ripe	2 weeks	
Dried fruit	6 months	2-4 days[+]	
Frozen fruit			1 year
Fruit juice concentrate		6 days	1 year
Fruit pies, baked		2-3 days	8 months
Grapes	Until ripe	5 days	
Melons	Until ripe	5 days	
Nectarines	Until ripe	5 days	
Peaches	Until ripe	5 days	1 year
Pears	Until ripe	5 days	1 year
Pineapple	Until ripe	5-7 days	1 year
Plums	Until ripe	5 days	
Dairy Products			
Butter		1-2 months	9 months
Buttermilk		2 weeks	

Cottage cheese		1 week	3 months
Cream cheese		2 weeks	
Cream-light, heavy, half- and-half		3-4 days	1-4 months
Eggnog commercial		3-5 days	6 months
Margarine		4-5 months	12 months
Condensed, evaporated and dry milk	12-23 months^	8-20 days*	
Milk		8-20 days	
Ice cream and sherbet			2 months
Hard natural cheese (e.g. cheddar, swiss)		3-6 months 3-4 weeks*	6 months
Processed cheese		3-4 weeks	6-8 months
Soft cheese (e.g. brie)		1 week	6 months
Pudding		1-2 days*	
Snack dips		1 week*	
Sour cream		2 weeks	
Non-dairy whipped cream, canned		3 months	
Real whipped cream, canned		3-4 weeks	
Yogurt		2 weeks	1-2 months
Meats, Poultry, Eggs and Fish			
Meats			
Fresh beef and bison steaks		3-5 days	6-9 months
Fresh beef and bison roasts		3-5 days	9-12 months
Fresh pork chops		2-3 days	4-6 months
Fresh lamb chops		3-5 days	6-8 months
Fresh veal		1-2 days	4-6 months

Fresh ground meat (e.g. beef, bison, veal, lamb)		1-2 days	3-4 months
Cooked meat		2-3 days	2-3 months
Canned meat	1 year	3-4 days*	3-4 months
Ham, whole		1 week	1-2 months
Ham, canned	2 years	1 week*	3-4 months
Ham, canned "keep refrigerated"		6-9 months 3-5 days*	3-4 months
Shelf-stable unopened canned meat (e.g. chili, deviled ham, corn beef)	1 year	1week*	
Ham, cook before eating		1 week	
Ham, fully cooked		2 weeks 1 week*	
Ham, dry-cured	1 year	1 month	
Ham salad, store prepared or homemade		3-5 days	
Bacon		2 weeks 1 week*	1 month
Corned beef, uncooked		5-7 days	1-2 months
Restructured (flaked) meat products			9-12 months
Sausage, fresh		1-2 days	1-2 months
Smoked breakfast sausage links, patties		1 week	2 months
Sausage, smoked (e.g. Mettwurst)		1 week	1-2 months
Sausage, semi-dry (e.g. Summer sausage)		2-3 weeks*	6 months
Sausage, dry smoked (e.g. Pepperoni, jerky, dry Salami)	1 year	1 month*	6 months
Frankfurters, bologna		2 weeks 3-7 days*	1-2 months
Luncheon meat		2 weeks 3-5 days*	1 month

Meat gravies		1-2 days	2-3 months
TV beef and pork dinners			18 months#
Meat based casseroles		3-4 days	4 months
Variety meats (giblets, tongue, liver, heart, etc.)		1-2 days	3-4 months
Vinegar pickled meats (e.g. pickled pigs feet)	1 year^	2 weeks*	
Fish			
Breaded fish			4-6 months
Canned fish	1 year	1-2 days*	
Cooked fish or seafood		3-4 days	3 months
Lean fish (e.g. cod, flounder, haddock)		1-2 days	6 months
Fatty fish (e.g. bluefish, salmon, mackeral)		1-2 days	2-3 months
Dry pickled fish		3-4 weeks	
Smoked fish		2 weeks	4-5 weeks
Seafood-clams, crab, lobster in shell		2 days	3 months
Seafood-oysters and scallops		4-5 days	3-4 months
Seafood-shrimp		4-5 days	1 year
Seafood-shucked clams		4-5 days	3-6 months
Tuna salad, store prepared or homemade		3-5 days	
Poultry			
Chicken nuggets or patties		1-2 days	
Chicken livers		1-2 days	3 months
Chicken and poultry TV dinners			6 months
Canned poultry^	2-5 years	3-4 days*	4-6 weeks
Cooked poultry		2-3 days	4-6 months

Fresh poultry		1-2 days	1 year
Frozen poultry parts		1-2 days	6-9 months
Canned poultry		1 day	3 months
Poultry pies, stews, and gravies		1-2 days	6 months
Poultry salads, store prepared or homemade		3-5 days	
Poultry stuffing, cooked		3-4 days	1 month
Eggs			
Eggs, in shell		3-5 weeks	
Eggs, hard-boiled		1 week	
Eggs, pasteurized		10 days 3 days*	1 year
Egg substitute		10 days 3 days*	1 year
Egg yolks (covered in water)		2-4 days	1 year
Egg whites (For each cup of egg yolk add 1 Tbs. of sugar or salt)		2-4 days	1 year
Wild Game			
Frog legs		1 day	6-9 months
Game birds		2 days	9 months
Small game (rabbit, squirrel, etc.)		2 days	9-12 months
Venison ground meat		1-2 days	2-3 months
Venison steaks and roasts		3-5 days	9-12 months
* Opened + Cooked ^ Refrigerate after opening # After manufacture date			

References

American Meat Institute Foundation. 1994. Yellow pages: answers to predictable questions consumers ask about meat and poultry. American Meat Institute Foundation, Washington, D.C.

Food Marketing Institute. 1999. The food keeper. Food Marketing Institute, Washington, D.C.

Freeland-Graves, J.H. and G.C. Peckham. 1996. Foundations of food preparation, 6th ed. Prentice-Hall, Inc. Englewood Cliffs, NJ.

Hillers, V.N. 1993. Storing foods at home. Washington State University Cooperative Extension, Pullman, WA. Publ. EB 1205.

National Restaurant Association. 2001. Be cool-chill out! Refrigerate promptly. National Restaurant Association Education Foundation¼s International Food Safety Council, Washington, D.C.

USDA. 1997. Basics for handling food safely. U.S. Department of Agriculture, Food Safety and Inspection Service, Washington, D.C.

Originally written by: Tim Roberts, Assistant Professor and Extension Specialist, Food Safety, Department of Human Nutrition, Foods and Exercise, Virginia Tech; Paul Graham, Associate Professor and Extension Specialist, Muscle Foods, Department of Food Science and Technology, Virginia Tech

---

Issued in furtherance of Cooperative Extension work, Virginia Polytechnic Institute and State University, Virginia State University, and the U.S. Department of Agriculture cooperating. Alan L. Grant, Dean, College of Agriculture and Life Sciences; Edwin J. Jones, Director, Virginia Cooperative Extension, Virginia Tech, Blacksburg; Jewel E. Hairston, Administrator, 1890 Extension Program, Virginia State, Petersburg.

May 1, 2009

*Source: http://pubs.ext.vt.edu/348/348-960/348-960.html Accessed: Jan. 9, 2013

Appendix B – Non-Food Storage Guidelines for Consumers

Item	Shelf Life
Alcohol, drinking	Indefinitely
Alcohol, rubbing	Indefinitely
Baby Wipes	1 year
Bags, Plastic, Lawn	Indefinitely
Bags, Plastic, Ziploc ®	Indefinitely
Bandages, Adhesive Strip	5 years
Bandages, Elastic (Ace® type)	6 – 7 years
Bandages, Gauze Pads	Indefinitely
Batteries, Alkaline	Expiration Date
Bleach	Indefinitely
Bug Spray	5 years
Candles	Indefinitely
Can Opener, Manual	Indefinitely
Cat Litter, Clay	Indefinitely
Cleansers, Household	10 years
Clothesline	Indefinitely
Clothespins	Indefinitely
Clothing, Socks	Indefinitely
Clothing, Underwear	Indefinitely
Conditioner, Hair	5 years
Containers, Plastic, Sealable	Indefinitely
Cord, Nylon	Indefinitely
Cotton Balls	Indefinitely
Cotton Swabs	Indefinitely
Dental Floss	Indefinitely
Deodorant / Antiperspirant	3 years
Detergent, Liquid, Clothing	Indefinitely
Detergent, Liquid, Dish	3 years
Detergent, Powdered	5 years
Diapers, Cloth	Indefinitely
Diapers, Disposable	Indefinitely
Flashlights (NOT Batteries)	Indefinitely
Foil, Aluminum, Heavy Duty	Indefinitely
Fuel, Cookstove	5 years
Fuel, Lantern	5 years
Gloves, Heavy Rubber, Utility	Indefinitely
Gloves, Latex	5 years
Grinder, Wheat, Manual	Indefinitely
Hand Sanitizer, Regular	4 years
Hydrogen Peroxide	3 years
Infant Bottles and Rings	Indefinitely

Ladies' Sanitary Supplies	Indefinitely
Lantern and Mantles	Indefinitely
Light Sticks, Chemical	3 – 12 months
Lotion, Calamine	2 years
Matches	5 years
Medicine, Analgesics	Expiration Date
Medicine, Antacids	Expiration Date
Medicines, Anti-Diarrheal	Expiration Date
Medicines, Anti-Histamine	Expiration Date
Medicines, Cough Drops	5 years
Medicines, Cough Syrup	Expiration Date
Medicines, Ipecac Syrup	Expiration Date
Medicines, Medamucil®	2 years
Medicines, Nasal Sprays	Expiration Date
Medicines, Prescriptions	Expiration Date
Medicines, Sambucol®	Expiration Date
Medicines, Zinc Lozenges	2 years
Oil, Motor, Detergent	3 years
Oil, Motor, Non-Detergent	Indefinitely
Oil, Two-Cycle	Indefinitely
Ointment, Antibacterial	1 year
Paper, Parchment	Indefinitely
Paper, Waxed	Indefinitely
Pet Food	Expiration Date
Petroleum Jelly	Indefinitely
Plastic Wrap	Indefinitely
Radio (NOT Batteries)	Indefinitely
Razors, Blades	Indefinitely
Razors, Disposable	Indefinitely
Safety Pins	Indefinitely
Scouring Pads	Indefinitely
Seeds, Garden	5 years
Shampoo	2 years
Shaving Cream, Can	2 years
Shaving Cream, Brushless	4 years
Soap, Anti-Bacterial	Indefinitely
Soap, Regular	Indefinitely
Splints	Indefinitely
Sunscreen	Expiration Date
Talcum Powder	Indefinitely
Tape, Duct	5 years
Tape, First Aid, Adhesive	4 years
Tape, Packaging	10 years
Thermometer, Medical, Traditional	Indefinitely
Toilet Paper	Indefinitely

Toothbrushes	Indefinitely
Toothpaste	3 years
Tooth Powder	Indefinitely
Tweezers	Indefinitely
Water Filters	Indefinitely
Water Purification Tablets	Indefinitely
WD40 Spray	Indefinitely

Appendix C – Food and Non-Food Tracking Chart

Item & Quantity	Date Purchased	Date Finished	Yearly Consumption

Food and Non-Food Tracking Chart

Item & Quantity	Date Purchased	Date Finished	Yearly Consumption

Appendix D – Food and Non-Food Inventory

Item	Optimal Quantity	Quantity On Hand	Expiration Date	Quantity Needed

Food and Non-Food Inventory

Item	Optimal Quantity	Quantity On Hand	Expiration Date	Quantity Needed

Appendix E – Faraday Cages

Faraday cage

From Wikipedia, the free encyclopedia*

A **Faraday cage** or **Faraday shield** is an enclosure formed by conducting material or by a mesh of such material. Such an enclosure blocks external static and non-static electric fields. Faraday cages are named after the English scientist Michael Faraday, who invented them in 1836.

A Faraday cage's operation depends on the fact that an external static electrical field causes the electric charges within the cage's conducting material to be distributed such that they cancel the field's effect in the cage's interior. This phenomenon is used, for example, to protect electronic equipment from lightning strikes and electrostatic discharges.

Faraday cages cannot block static and slowly varying magnetic fields, such as the Earth's magnetic field (a compass will still work inside). To a large degree, though, they shield the interior from external electromagnetic radiation if the conductor is thick enough and any holes are significantly smaller than the wavelength of the radiation. For example, certain computer forensic test procedures of electronic systems that require an environment free of electromagnetic interference can be carried out within a *screen room*. These rooms are spaces that are completely enclosed by one or more layers of a fine metal mesh or perforated sheet metal. The metal layers are grounded in order to dissipate any electric currents generated from external or internal electromagnetic fields, and thus they block a large amount of the electromagnetic interference. See also electromagnetic shielding.

The reception or transmission of radio waves, a form of electromagnetic radiation, to or from an antenna within a Faraday cage are heavily attenuated or blocked by a Faraday cage.

History

In 1836, Michael Faraday observed that the charge on a charged conductor resided only on its exterior and had no influence on anything enclosed within it. To demonstrate this fact, he built a room coated with metal foil and allowed high-voltage discharges from an electrostatic generator to strike the outside of the room. He used an electroscope to show that there was no electric charge present on the inside of the room's walls.

Although this cage effect has been attributed to Michael Faraday, it was Benjamin Franklin in 1755 who observed the effect by lowering an uncharged cork ball suspended on a silk thread through an opening in an electrically charged metal can. In his words, "the cork was not attracted to the inside of the can as it would have been to the outside, and though it touched the bottom, yet when drawn out it was not found to be electrified (charged) by that touch, as it would have been by touching the outside. The fact is singular." Franklin had discovered the behavior of what we now refer to as a Faraday cage or shield (based on one of Faraday's famous ice pail experiments which duplicated Franklin's cork and can).

Operation

An external electrical field causes the charges to rearrange, which cancels the field inside.

A Faraday cage is best understood as an approximation to an ideal hollow conductor. Externally or internally applied electromagnetic fields produce forces on the charge carriers (usually electrons) within the conductor; the charges are redistributed accordingly (that is, electric currents are generated). Once the charges have rearranged so as to cancel the applied field inside, the currents stop.

If a charge is placed inside an ungrounded Faraday cage, the internal face of the cage becomes charged (in the same manner described for an external charge) to prevent the existence of a field inside the body of the cage. However, this charging of the inner face re-distributes the charges in the body of the cage. This charges the outer face of the cage with a charge equal in sign and magnitude to the one placed inside the cage. Since the internal charge and the inner face cancel each other out, the spread of charges on the outer face is not affected by the position of the internal charge inside the cage. So for all intents and purposes, the cage generates the same DC electric field that it would generate if it were simply affected by the charge placed inside. The same is not true for electromagnetic waves.

If the cage is grounded, the excess charges will go to the ground instead of the outer face, so the inner face and the inner charge will cancel each other out and the rest of the cage will retain a neutral charge.

Effectiveness of shielding of a static electric field depends upon the geometry of the conductive material. In the case of a nonlinear varying electric field, and hence an accompanying varying magnetic field, the faster the variations are (i.e., the higher the frequencies), the better the material resists penetration, but on the other hand, the better it passes through a mesh of given size. In this case the shielding also depends on the electrical conductivity of the conductive materials used in the cages, as well as their thicknesses.

Examples

- A microwave oven is an example of an inside out Faraday cage, keeping the RF energy within the cage rather than keeping it out.

- Elevators and other rooms with metallic conducting frames famously simulate a Faraday cage effect, leading to a loss of signal and "dead zones" for users of cellular phones, radios, and other electronic devices that require electromagnetic external signals. Small, physical Faraday cages are used by electronics engineers during testing to simulate such an environment in order to make sure that the device gracefully handles these conditions.

- The shield of a screened cable, such as USB cables or the coaxial cable used for cable television, protects the internal conductors from external electrical noise and prevents the RF signals from leaking out.

- A booster bag (shopping bag lined with aluminum foil) acts as a Faraday cage. It is often used by shoplifters to steal RFID-tagged items.

- Plastic bags are included with electronic toll collection devices which are impregnated with metal to allow motorists to place them in the bag so that a toll charge is not registered or a device will not register a charge while being shipped to a customer's home after ordering in a delivery truck.

- Some electrical linemen wear Faraday suits, which allow them to work on live, high voltage power lines without risk of electrocution. The suit prevents electrical current from flowing through the body, and has no theoretical voltage limit. Linemen have successfully worked even the highest voltage (Kazakhstan's Ekibastuz–Kokshetau line 1150 kV) lines safely.

- The scan room of a Magnetic Resonance Imaging (MRI) machine is designed as a Faraday cage. This prevents external RF (radio frequency) signals from being added to data collected from the patient, which would affect the resulting image. Radiographers are trained to identify the characteristic artifacts created on images should the Faraday cage be damaged.

- Faraday cages are routinely used in analytical chemistry to reduce noise while making sensitive measurements. A home-made Faraday cage used for simultaneous microscopy and electrochemistry is shown to the right.

*http://en.wikipedia.org/wiki/Faraday_cage Accessed: Jan. 10, 2013

Appendix F – Survival Communications

Perhaps you have prepared for WTSHTF or TEOTWAWKI with respect to food, water, self-defense and shelter. But what about communication?

Whenever there is a disaster (hurricane, earthquake, economic collapse, nuclear war, EMF, solar eruption, etc.), the normal means of communication that we're all reliant upon (cell phone, land line phone, the Internet, etc.) will probably be, at best, sporadic and at worst, non-existent.

As this author sees it, short of smoke signals and mirrors, there are three options for communication in "trying times": (1) GMRS or FRS radios; (2) CB radios; and (3) ham or amateur radio. Let's consider each of these options to come up with the most acceptable one.

GMRS (General Mobile Radio Service) / FRS (Family Radio Service)

GMRS (General Mobile Radio Service) / FRS (Family Radio Service) radios work optimally over short distances where there is minimal interference. Originally designed to be used as pagers, particularly inside a building or other such confined area, these radios are low-cost and convenient to carry. Unfortunately their small size and light weight comes with a trade-off – short range and short battery life. These radios are supposed to be able to communicate for up to 25-30 miles. Right. That's on level terrain, without buildings or trees getting in the way. While battery life technology is constantly improving, you will need spare batteries to keep communicating or someway of recharging the ones in the radio. In this author's opinion, GMRS/FRS radios are not first choice when concerned with medium or long range communication.

CB (Citizens Band)

CB (Citizens Band) radios operate in a frequency range originally reserved for ham or amateur radio operation. Because of the overwhelming number of people wishing quick, low-cost, regulation-free communication, the FCC (Federal Communication Commission) split off a portion of the frequency spectrum and allowed anyone to purchase a CB radio and start communicating. No test. No license. Just personal/business communication. Today, CB radios are readily available in such outlets as eBay and Craigslist. This author has seen them at yard/garage/tag sales and at flea markets.

CB radios come in a variety of "flavors." Fixed units, sometimes referred to as base units are intended for home use. For the most part, they derive their power from the utility company. In the event of loss of electricity, most base units can also be connected to a 12-volt battery, like that in your car/truck. If you choose to obtain a fixed unit, make sure you know how to connect the unit to the battery – ahead of time. Trying to figure this out when you're under extra stress is not a good situation.

A second type of CB radio is designed to be mobile, that is, installed in your car/truck. It gets its power from the vehicle's battery. You can either attach an antenna permanently to the vehicle or have a removable, magnetic type antenna.

The third type of CB radio is designed for handheld use. They are small and light. Most weigh less than a pound and operate on batteries. Yes, using batteries in a CB poses the same limitations as those by the GMRS/FRS radios, but have the added advantage that most handheld units come with a cigarette lighter adapter. Comes in handy when you are on the move and wish to be able to communicate both from a vehicle and also when you have to abandon it.

While they have a greater range than GMRS/FRS radios, CB radios are, legally, limited to operate on 40 channels, with a power rating of four (4) watts or less. Yes, it is possible to alter CB radios to get around these limitations, but not legally,

Ham/Amateur Radio

Ham/Amateur radio is very appealing. With a ham radio, you are not limited to less than 50 miles, but can communicate with anyone in the world (who also has access to a ham radio, of course).

What follows is a list of books on Survival Communications by John E. Parnell. In his books, the author tells how one might become a FCC licensed amateur radio operator (about the required exam, cost of taking the exam, where to take the exam, etc.). In addition, Parnell also suggests places where amateur radio equipment might be purchased at a reasonable cost. He also covers such topics as call signs, and third-party communications.

Knowing that while everybody might see the value of amateur radio, not everybody can / wants to become licensed. An important part of Parnell's books is that therein he lists all of the licensed amateur radio operators in each state, sorted by city, sub-sorted by street name, and then sub-sub-sorted by house number. In that way, a person in a crisis may look in one of his books for those people who are close to the crisis, those who are already prepared communication-wise. The number of licensed operators listed range from about 500 to over 25,000, depending upon the size of the state / region. Every state is covered. Larger states, e.g., California, Texas, New York, etc., have more than one book covering the state.

The books are available in both English and Spanish, bound book or PDF form. They may be purchased either from the reader's favorite online or brick-and-mortar bookstore, or directly from the publisher:

Tutor Turtle Press, LLC
1027 S. Pendleton St., Suite B-10
Easley, SC 29642
(864) 553-1533

www.TurtorTurtlePress.com

Title of Book	13-ISBN Number
Survival Communications in Alabama	978-1478308256

Supervivencia las Communicacionesncia en Alabama	978-1625122117
Survival Communications in Alaska	978-1478172901
Supervivencia las Communicacionesncia en Alaska	978-1625122124
Survival Communications in Arizona: Colorado Plateau Region	978-1625120021
Supervivencia las Communicacionesncia en Arizona: Región central	978-1625122131
Survival Communications in Arizona: Transition Zone and Basin & Range Region	978-1625120014
Supervivencia las Communicacionesncia en Arizona: Región occidental	978-1625122148
Survival Communications in Arkansas	978-1478147794
Supervivencia las Communicacionesncia en Arkansas	978-1625122155
Survival Communications in California: Bay Delta Region	978-1625120113
Supervivencia las Communicacionesncia en California: Región Bay Delta	978-1625122162
Survival Communications in California: Central Region	978-1625120069
Supervivencia las Communicacionesncia en California: Región central	978-1625122179
Survival Communications in California: Inland Desserts Region	978-1625120076
Supervivencia las Communicacionesncia en California: Desiertos del interior	978-1625122186
Survival Communications in California: North Bay Delta Region	978-1625122063

Comunicaciones de supervivencia en California: Región Bay Delta	978-1625122247
Survival Communications in California: North Central Region	978-1625122070
Comunicaciones de supervivencia en California: Región central	978-1625122254
Survival Communications in California: Northern Region	978-1625122087
Comunicaciones de supervivencia en California: Región central al norte	978-1625122261
Survival Communications in California: Los Angeles County - Supervisory Region - District 1	978-1625122094
Supervivencia las Communicacionesncia en California: Costa al sur condado LA– Región supervisorial 1	978-1625122193
Survival Communications in California: Los Angeles County - Supervisory Region - District 2	978-1625120120
Supervivencia las Communicacionesncia en California: Costa al sur condado LA– Región supervisorial 2	978-1625122209
Survival Communications in California: Los Angeles County - Supervisory Region - District 3	978-1625120137
Supervivencia las Communicacionesncia en California: Costa al sur condado LA– Región supervisorial 3	978-1625122216
Survival Communications in California: Los Angeles County - Supervisory Region - District 4	978-1625120144
Supervivencia las Communicacionesncia en California: Costa al sur condado LA– Región supervisorial 4	978-1625122224
Survival Communications in California: Los Angeles County - Supervisory Region - District 5	978-1625120151

Supervivencia las Communicacionesncia en California: Costa al sur condado LA– Región supervisorial 5	978-1625122230
Survival Communications in California: South Coast Orange County Region	978-1625120168
Supervivencia las Communicacionesncia en California: Costa al sur – Región condado Orange	978-1625122278
Survival Communications in California: South Coast San Diego Region	978-1625120175
Supervivencia las Communicacionesncia en California: Costa al sur – Región San Diego	978-1625122285
Survival Communications in California: Southern Region - Santa Barbara Ventura	978-1625120182
Supervivencia las Communicacionesncia en California: Costa al sur – Regiones Santa Barbara y Ventura	978-1625122292
Survival Communications in Colorado	978-1479242634
Supervivencia las Communicacionesncia en Colorado	978-1625122308
Survival Communications in Connecticut	978-1625120199
Supervivencia las Communicacionesncia en Connecticut	978-1625122315
Survival Communications in Delaware	978-1478191605
Supervivencia las Communicacionesncia en Delaware	978-1625122322
Survival Communications in Florida: Emerald Coast and Big Bend Regions	978-1479116041
Supervivencia las Communicacionesncia en Florida: Región costa esmeralda	978-1625122339
Survival Communications in Florida: North Florida and Heart of Florida Regions	978-1479117727

Supervivencia las Communicacionesncia en Florida: Regiones FL al norte y corazón de FL	978-1625122353
Survival Communications in Florida: Space Coast Region	978-1479119707
Supervivencia las Communicacionesncia en Florida: Región costa espacio	978-1625122360
Survival Communications in Florida: Sun Coast Region	978-1479135592
Supervivencia las Communicacionesncia en Florida: Región costa del sol	978-1625122377
Survival Communications in Florida: Gold Coast Region	978-1479132249
Supervivencia las Communicacionesncia en Florida: Región costa dorada	978-1625122346
Survival Communications in Florida: Treasure Coast Region	978-1479135936
Supervivencia las Communicacionesncia en Florida: Región costa tesoro	978-1625122384
Survival Communications in Georgia: North Region	978-1479255221
Supervivencia las Communicacionesncia en Georgia: Región al norte	978-1625122391
Survival Communications in Georgia: South Region	978-1479255306
Supervivencia las Communicacionesncia en Georgia: Región al sur	978-1625122407
Survival Communications in Hawaii	978-1478199106
Supervivencia las Communicacionesncia en Hawai	978-1625122414

Survival Communications in Idaho	978-1478169840
Supervivencia las Communicacionesncia en Idaho	978-1625122421
Survival Communications in Illinois: Chicagoland	1625120052
Supervivencia las Communicacionesncia en Illinois: Región Chicagoland	978-1625122438
Survival Communications in Illinois: Downstate	978-1625120038
Supervivencia las Communicacionesncia en Illinois: Región Downstate	978-1625122445
Survival Communications in Indiana: North Region	978-1625120083
Supervivencia las Communicacionesncia en Indiana: Región al norte	978-1625122452
Survival Communications in Indiana: South Region	978-1625120090
Supervivencia las Communicacionesncia en Indiana: Región al sur	978-1625122469
Survival Communications in Iowa	978-1478288831
Supervivencia las Communicacionesncia en Iowa	978-1625122476
Survival Communications in Kansas	978-1478254034
Supervivencia las Communicacionesncia en Kansas	978-1625122483
Survival Communications in Kentucky	978-1478251576
Supervivencia las Communicacionesncia en Kentucky	978-1625122490
Survival Communications in Louisiana	978-1478274285
Supervivencia las Communicacionesncia en Louisiana	978-1625122506
Survival Communications in Maine	978-1625120403
Supervivencia las Communicacionesncia en Maine	978-1625122513
Survival Communications in Maryland	978-1479136865
Supervivencia las Communicacionesncia en Maryland	978-1625122520

Survival Communications in Massachusetts	978-1625120427
Supervivencia las Communicacionesncia en Massachusetts	978-1625122537
Survival Communications in Michigan: North and East Regions	978-1625120434
Supervivencia las Communicacionesncia en Michigan: Regiones al norte y al este	978-1625122544
Survival Communications in Michigan: South West Region	978-1625120441
Supervivencia las Communicacionesncia en Michigan: Región al sudoeste	978-1625122551
Survival Communications in Minnesota	978-1479262717
Supervivencia las Communicacionesncia en Minnesota	978-1625122568
Survival Communications in Mississippi	978-1478169963
Supervivencia las Communicacionesncia en Mississippi	978-1625122575
Survival Communications in Missouri	978-1479158492
Supervivencia las Communicacionesncia en Missouri	978-1625122582
Survival Communications in Montana	978-1478174554
Supervivencia las Communicacionesncia en Montana	978-1625122599
Survival Communications in Nebraska	978-1478286806
Supervivencia las Communicacionesncia en Nebraska	978-1625122605
Survival Communications in Nevada	978-1478230816
Supervivencia las Communicacionesncia en Nevada	978-1625122612
Survival Communications in New Hampshire	978-1625120519
Supervivencia las Communicacionesncia en New Hampshire	978-1625122629

Survival Communications in New Jersey	978-1479312535
Supervivencia las Communicacionesncia en New Jersey	978-1625122636
Survival Communications in New Mexico	978-1478285601
Supervivencia las Communicacionesncia en New México	978-1625122643
Survival Communications in New York: Capital District - East	978-1479151738
Supervivencia las Communicacionesncia en New York: Distrito capital– región al este	978-1625122650
Survival Communications in New York: Central Region	978-1479151783
Supervivencia las Communicacionesncia en New York: Distrito central	978-1625122667
Survival Communications in New York: Mid-Hudson and Westchester Regions	978-1479151806
Supervivencia las Communicacionesncia en New York: Mid-Hudson y región Westchester	978-1625122674
Survival Communications in New York: Western Region	978-1479151820
supervivencia Comunicaciones en New York: Región Occidental	978-1625122698
Survival Communications in New York: NYC - Long Island Region	978-1479151882
Supervivencia Comunicaciones en New York: NYC - Región Isla Larga	978-1625122681
Survival Communications in North Carolina: Coastal Region	978-1478133001
Supervivencia las Communicacionesncia en Carolina del Norte: Región costera	978-1625122704

Survival Communications in North Carolina: Mountain Region	978-1478118503
Supervivencia las Communicacionesncia en Carolina del Norte: Región de las montañas	978-1625122711
Survival Communications in North Carolina: Piedmont Region	978-1478121350
Supervivencia las Communicacionesncia en Carolina del Norte: Región del Piamonte	978-1625122728
Survival Communications in North Dakota	978-1478176145
Supervivencia las Communicacionesncia en Dakota del Norte	
Survival Communications in Ohio: Central Region	978-1479244256
Supervivencia las Communicacionesncia en Ohio: Región central	978-1625122735
Survival Communications in Ohio: North East Region	978-1479244287
Supervivencia las Communicacionesncia en Ohio: Región nordeste	978-1625122759
Survival Communications in Ohio: North West Region	978-1479244324
Supervivencia las Communicacionesncia en Ohio: Región del noroeste	978-1625122766
Survival Communications in Ohio: South East Region	978-1479244348
Supervivencia las Communicacionesncia en Ohio: Región del sudeste	978-1625122773
Survival Communications in Ohio: South West Region	978-1479244393
Supervivencia las Communicacionesncia en Ohio: Región del sudoeste	978-1625122780

Survival Communications in Oklahoma	978-1479191062
Supervivencia las Communicacionesncia en Oklahoma	978-1625122797
Survival Communications in Oregon: Eastern Region	978-1625120045
Supervivencia las Communicacionesncia en Oregon: Región del este	978-1625122803
Survival Communications in Oregon: Western Region	978-1625120007
Supervivencia las Communicacionesncia en Oregon: Región del oeste	978-1625122810
Survival Communications in Pennsylvania: Central Region	978-1625120717
Supervivencia las Communicacionesncia en Pennsylvania: Región central	978-1625122827
Survival Communications in Pennsylvania: Eastern Region	978-1625120724
Supervivencia las Communicacionesncia en Pennsylvania: Región del este	978-1625122834
Survival Communications in Pennsylvania: Western Region	978-1625120731
Supervivencia las Communicacionesncia en Pennsylvania: Región del oeste	978-1625122841
Survival Communications in Rhode Island	978-1475191288
Supervivencia las Communicacionesncia en Rhode Island	978-1625122858
Survival Communications in South Carolina	978-1475084788
Supervivencia las Communicacionesncia en Carolina del Sur	978-1625122865
Survival Communications in South Dakota	978-1478172536

Supervivencia las Communicacionesncia en Dakota del Sur	978-1625122872
Survival Communications in Tennessee: East Region	978-1478305712
Supervivencia las Communicacionesncia en Tennessee: Región del este	978-1625122889
Survival Communications in Tennessee: Middle Region	978-1478292968
Supervivencia las Communicacionesncia en Tennessee: Región central	978-1625122896
Survival Communications in Tennessee: West Region	978-1478291336
Supervivencia las Communicacionesncia en Tennessee: Región del oeste	978-1625122902
Survival Communications in Texas: Big Bend Region	978-1477478486
Supervivencia las Communicacionesncia en Texas: Región Big Bend	978-1625122919
Survival Communications in Texas: East Texas Piney Woods Region	978-1477478578
Supervivencia las Communicacionesncia en Texas: Tejas del este y región Piney Woods	978-1625122926
Survival Communications in Texas: Gulf Coast Region	978-1477478608
Supervivencia las Communicacionesncia en Texas: Región de la Costa Golfo	978-1625122933
Survival Communications in Texas: Hill Country Region	978-1477478646
Supervivencia las Communicacionesncia en Texas: Región Hill Country	978-1625122940

Survival Communications in Texas: Panhandle Plains Region	978-1477478660
Supervivencia las Communicacionesncia en Texas: Región Panhandle y llanura	978-1625122964
Survival Communications in Texas: North Prairies & Lakes Region	978-1477522110
Supervivencia las Communicacionesncia en Texas: Región de las praderas del norte y lagos	978-1625122957
Survival Communications in Texas: South Prairies & Lakes Region	978-1477522189
Supervivencia las Communicacionesncia en Texas: Praderas del sur y región del lago	978-1625122971
Survival Communications in Texas: South Texas Plains Region	978-1477478714
Supervivencia las Communicacionesncia en Texas: Región de Tejas del sur y llanura	978-1625122988
Survival Communications in Utah	978-1475191264
Supervivencia las Communicacionesncia en Utah	978-1625122995
Survival Communications in Vermont	978-1475191394
Supervivencia las Communicacionesncia en Vermont	978-1625123008
Survival Communications in Virginia: Cities A - L	978-1625120908
Supervivencia las Communicacionesncia en Virginia: Región de la meseta Appalachian	978-1625123015
Survival Communications in Virginia: Cities M - Z	978-1625120922
Supervivencia las Communicacionesncia en Virginia: Región Blue Ridge	978-1625123022
Survival Communications in Washington: Eastern and Central Regions	978-1479174584

Supervivencia las Communicacionesncia en Washington: Regiones central y del este	978-1625123039
Survival Communications in Washington: Northwest Region	978-1479174720
Supervivencia las Communicacionesncia en Washington: Región noroeste	978-1625123046
Survival Communications in Washington: Southwest Region	978-1479174829
Supervivencia las Communicacionesncia en Washington: Región del sudoeste	978-1625123053
Survival Communications in West Virginia	978-1478318873
Supervivencia las Communicacionesncia en West Virginia	978-1625123060
Survival Communications in Wisconsin	978-1477664902
Supervivencia las Communicacionesncia en Wisconsin	978-1625123077
Survival Communications in Wyoming	978-1478159285
Supervivencia las Communicacionesncia en Wyoming	978-1625123084
Survival Communications in the District of Columbia	978-147139300
Supervivencia las Comunicaciones en el Distrito de Columbia	978-1625123091

Appendix G – Home Inventory Records

Living room

Item	Description (Mfr/Brand Name & Serial/Model No.)	Purchase Date	Original Cost	Replacement Cost	Expected Life	Depreciation	Actual Cash Value
Air conditioner (window)							
Bookcases (not fastened to walls)							
Books* (p. 34)							
Knickknacks * (p. 44)							
Cassette tape player, cassette tapes* (p. 35)							
Ceiling fans							
Chairs							
Couches, sofas, sectionals							
Clocks							
Coffee tables							
Compact disc player, CDs* (p. 35)							
Curtains or drapes							
Desk and contents							
End tables							
Fireplace tools, screen, grate							
Footstools							
Lamps (hanging, floor, light fixtures)							
Mirrors							
Musical instruments* (p. 48)							

*List in special inventory section.
Living room inventory continued on next page.

141

Living room, continued

Item	Description (Mfr/Brand Name & Serial/Model No.)	Purchase Date	Original Cost	Replacement Cost	Expected Life	Depreciation	Actual Cash Value
Organ/piano and bench							
Photograph albums* (p. 47)							
Pictures, prints, wall hangings* (p. 47)							
Pillows							
Plants/flower arrangements							
Radios/receivers/equalizers							
Rugs							
Stereo, turntable, speakers, record albums* (p. 35)							
Table lamps							
Telephones, answering machine							
Television							
Vases*							
VCR, videotapes* (p. 35)							
Wood-burning stove							
Other furniture:							
Total							

* List in special inventory section.

Living room 7

Dining room

Item	Description (Mfr/Brand Name & Serial/Model No.)	Purchase Date	Original Cost	Replacement Cost	Expected Life	Depreciation	Actual Cash Value
Air conditioner (window)							
Buffet							
Candlestick holders/candelabra							
Chairs and dining chairs							
China* (p. 44)							
China cabinet/hutch							
Clocks							
Crystal* (p. 44)							
Curtains and/or drapes							
Dining table							
Electric appliances* (p. 43)							
Flatware* (p. 44)							
Glassware* (p. 44)							
Knickknacks* (p. 44)							
Lamps (floor or hanging)							
Mirrors (portable)							
Pictures, prints, wall hangings* (p. 47)							
Plants/flower arrangements							
Rugs							

*List in special inventory section.
Dining room inventory continued on next page.

143

Dining room, continued

Item	Description (Mfr/Brand Name & Serial/Model No.)	Purchase Date	Original Cost	Replacement Cost	Expected Life	Depreciation	Actual Cash Value
Silverware* (p. 44)							
Tables							
Table linens, placemats, napkins, napkin holders* (p. 50)							
Telephones							
Vases* (p. 44)							
Wines, liquors							
Other furniture:							
Total							

*List in special inventory section.

Kitchen/breakfast nook

Item	Description (Mfr/Brand Name & Serial/Model No.)	Purchase Date	Original Cost	Replacement Cost	Expected Life	Depreciation	Actual Cash Value
Air conditioner (window)							
Baby high chair							
Butcher block/baker's rack							
Cabinets (not fastened to walls)							
Canisters, cookie jar, oil bottles							
Chairs							
Clock							
Coffeemaker/grinder							
Cookbooks							
Cutlery, flatware* (p. 44)							
Cutting boards							
Dishes* (p. 44)							
Dishwasher							
Electrical appliances (toaster, frying pan, waffle iron, hand mixer, pasta machine, ice-cream maker, etc.)							
Freezer							

*List in special inventory section.
Kitchen/breakfast nook inventory continued on next page.

145

Kitchen/breakfast nook, continued

Item	Description (Mfr/Brand Name & Serial/Model No.)	Purchase Date	Original Cost	Replacement Cost	Expected Life	Depreciation	Actual Cash Value
Garbage disposal							
Kitchen utensils (rubber spatulas, whisks, cookie cutters, rolling pins, measuring spoons and cups, Tupperware, etc.)							
Knives/knife holder* (p. 44)							
Microwave oven							
Oven/cooktop							
Picnic baskets							
Pictures, prints, wall hangings* (p. 47)							
Pots, pans, cookware							
Radio							
Refrigerator							
Rugs or carpet							
Serving bowls/platters/pitchers							
Spice rack							
Staple foods							
Table linens, placemats, napkins, napkin holders* (p. 50)							
Tables							
Tea kettle							

*List in special inventory section.
Kitchen/breakfast nook inventory continued on next page.

Kitchen/breakfast nook   11

Kitchen/breakfast nook, continued

Item	Description (Mfr/Brand Name & Serial/Model No.)	Purchase Date	Original Cost	Replacement Cost	Expected Life	Depreciation	Actual Cash Value
Telephone							
Television							
Toaster oven							
Towels* (p. 33)							
Trash compactor							
Vases* (p. 44)							
Wine rack							
Total							

Laundry room

Item	Description (Mfr/Brand Name & Serial/Model No.)	Purchase Date	Original Cost	Replacement Cost	Expected Life	Depreciation	Actual Cash Value
Broom, mop, bucket, dustpan							
Cabinets (not attached to walls)							
Dryer							
Folding table							
Freezer							
Laundry baskets							
Refrigerator							
Sewing machine							
Iron and ironing board							
Vacuum cleaner, cleaning equipment							
Washing machine							
Water heater							
Water softener							
Rugs or carpet							
Total							

Master bedroom

Item	Description (Mfr/Brand Name & Serial/Model No.)	Purchase Date	Original Cost	Replacement Cost	Expected Life	Depreciation	Actual Cash Value
Air conditioner (window)							
Aquarium							
Bed frames							
Bedspreads, blankets* (p. 33)							
Books* (p. 34)							
Bookcases (not fastened to walls)							
Ceiling fan							
Chaise longue/ love seat							
Chest of drawers, dressers							
Chairs							
Clocks							
Clothes hamper							
Clothing* (pp. 37–41)							
Curtains or drapes							
Desk							
Dressing screens							
Hope chest							
Humidifier							
Jewelry* (p. 45)							

*List in special inventory section.
Master bedroom inventory continued on next page.

149

Master bedroom, continued

Item	Description (Mfr/Brand Name & Serial/Model No.)	Purchase Date	Original Cost	Replacement Cost	Expected Life	Depreciation	Actual Cash Value
Knickknacks* (p. 44)							
Lamps							
Mattresses, box springs							
Mirrors (not fixed to walls)							
Night stands, tables							
Pictures, prints, wall hangings* (p. 47)							
Pillows, quilts* (p. 33)							
Plants/flowers							
Radio							
Rocking chair							
Rugs							
Sheets, pillowcases* (p. 33)							
Stereo, CD player, CDs* (p. 35)							
Telephone							
Television, VCR, videotapes* (p. 35)							
Vanity table							
Vases* (p. 44)							
Total							

*List in special inventory section.

Bedroom, second

Item	Description (Mfr/Brand Name & Serial/Model No.)	Purchase Date	Original Cost	Replacement Cost	Expected Life	Depreciation	Actual Cash Value
Air conditioner (window)							
Bed frames							
Bedspreads, blankets* (p. 33)							
Books* (p. 34)							
Bookcases (not fastened to walls)							
Chairs							
Chest of drawers, dressers							
Clocks							
Clotheshamper							
Clothing* (pp. 37–41)							
Curtains or drapes							
Desk							
Dressing screens							
Hope chest							
Humidifier							
Jewelry* (p. 45)							
Knickknacks* (p. 44)							
Lamps							
Mattresses, box springs							

*List in special inventory section.
Bedroom, second, inventory continued on next page.

151

Bedroom, second, continued

Item	Description (Mfr/Brand Name & Serial/Model No.)	Purchase Date	Original Cost	Replacement Cost	Expected Life	Depreciation	Actual Cash Value
Mirrors (not fastened to walls)							
Night stands, tables							
Pictures, prints, wall hangings* (p. 47)							
Pillows, quilts* (p. 33)							
Plants/flowers							
Radio							
Rugs							
Sewing machine							
Sheets, pillowcases* (p. 33)							
Stereo, CD player, CDs* (p. 35)							
Telephone							
Television, VCR, videotapes* (p. 35)							
Total							

*List in special inventory section.

Bedroom, third

Item	Description (Mfr./Brand Name & Serial/Model No.)	Purchase Date	Original Cost	Replacement Cost	Expected Life	Depreciation	Actual Cash Value
Air conditioner (window)							
Beds							
Bedspreads, blankets* (p. 33)							
Books* (p. 34)							
Bookcases (not fastened to walls)							
Chairs							
Chest of drawers, dressers							
Clocks							
Clothes hamper							
Clothing* (pp. 37–41)							
Curtains or drapes							
Desk							
Hope chest							
Humidifier							
Jewelry* (p. 45)							
Knickknacks* (p. 44)							
Lamps							
Mattresses, box springs							
Mirrors (not fastened to walls)							

*List in special inventory section.

Bedroom, third, continued

Item	Description (Mfr/Brand Name & Serial/Model No.)	Purchase Date	Original Cost	Replacement Cost	Expected Life	Depreciation	Actual Cash Value
Night stands, tables							
Pictures, prints, wall hangings* (p. 47)							
Pillows, quilts* (p. 33)							
Plants/flowers							
Radio							
Rugs							
Sewing machine							
Sheets, pillowcases* (p. 33)							
Stereo, CD player, CDs* (p. 35)							
Telephone							
Television, VCR, videotapes* (p. 35)							
Total							

*List in special inventory section.

154

Bedroom, fourth (baby's room)

Item	Description (Mfr/Brand Name & Serial/Model No.)	Purchase Date	Original Cost	Replacement Cost	Expected Life	Depreciation	Actual Cash Value
Baby swing							
Bed (bassinet or crib)							
Blankets* (p. 33)							
Bookcases (not attached to wall)							
Books* (p. 34)							
Car seat							
Chairs/rocking chair							
Changing table							
Chest of drawers, dressers							
Clock							
Clothing* (pp. 37–41)							
Curtains or drapes							
Humidifier							
Infant carrier/baby seat							
Lamps							
Linens* (p. 33)							
Mattress, box springs							
Mirrors (not fastened to walls)							
Mobiles							

*List in special inventory section.
Bedroom, fourth (baby's room), inventory continued on next page.

155

Bedroom, fourth (baby's room), continued

Item	Description (Mfr/Brand Name & Serial/Model No.)	Purchase Date	Original Cost	Replacement Cost	Expected Life	Depreciation	Actual Cash Value
Pictures, prints, wall hangings* (p. 47)							
Playpen							
Rocking chair							
Rocking horse							
Rugs							
Stroller							
Tables							
Toy chest							
Toys* (p. 36)							
Walker/exerciser							
Total							

*List in special inventory section.

Bedroom, fourth (baby's room)   21

Master bathroom

Item	Description (Mfr/Brand Name & Serial/Model No.)	Purchase Date	Original Cost	Replacement Cost	Expected Life	Depreciation	Actual Cash Value
Baskets, wicker							
Cabinets (not fastened to walls)							
Chairs							
Clothes hamper							
Contact lenses							
Cosmetics, toilet accessories							
Curtains							
Electrical appliances (hair dryer, razor, curling iron, electric rollers, toothbrush, etc.)							
Eyeglasses							
First aid kit							
Hearing aids							
Heating pad							
Iron and ironing board							
Knickknacks* (p. 44)							
Medicines (prescription and nonprescription)							
Mirrors (portable)							
Pictures, prints, wall hangings* (p. 47)							

*Master bathroom inventory continued on next page.

157

Master bathroom, continued

Item	Description (Mfr/Brand Name & Serial/Model No.)	Purchase Date	Original Cost	Replacement Cost	Expected Life	Depreciation	Actual Cash Value
Plants/flowers							
Radio							
Rugs, bath mats							
Scales							
Shelves (not attached)							
Shower curtain							
Soap dispensers, etc.							
Television							
Towels, sheets* (p. 33)							
Wastebasket							
Total							

Bathroom, second

Item	Description (Mfr/Brand Name & Serial/Model No.)	Purchase Date	Original Cost	Replacement Cost	Expected Life	Depreciation	Actual Cash Value
Baskets, wicker							
Cabinets (not fastened to walls)							
Clothes hamper							
Cosmetics							
Curtains							
Electric appliances (hair dryer, curling iron, electric rollers, toothbrush, etc.)							
First aid kit							
Heating pad							
Medicines (prescription and nonprescription)							
Mirrors (not fastened to walls)							
Radio							
Rugs							
Shower curtain							
Television							
Towels* (p. 33)							
Total							

Family room

Item	Description (Mfr/Brand Name & Serial/Model No.)	Purchase Date	Original Cost	Replacement Cost	Expected Life	Depreciation	Actual Cash Value
Air conditioner (window)							
Baskets							
Binoculars							
Board games* (p. 48)							
Books* (p. 34)							
Bookcases (not fastened to walls)							
Cassette tapes, compact discs, records* (p. 35)							
Ceiling fan							
Chairs, footstools							
Children's toys* (p. 36)							
Collections* (p. 48)							
Couches, sofas, sectionals							
Curtains, drapes							
Desk							
Entertainment center							
Exercise equipment* (p. 48)							
Fireplace tools, grate, screen							
Hobby equipment* (p. 48)							
Knickknacks* (p. 44)							

*List in special inventory section.
Family room inventory continued on next page.

Family room, continued

Item	Description (Mfr/Brand Name & Serial/Model No.)	Purchase Date	Original Cost	Replacement Cost	Expected Life	Depreciation	Actual Cash Value
Lamps							
Mementos							
Musical instruments* (p. 48)							
Photo albums* (p. 47)							
Pictures, prints, wall hangings* (p. 47)							
Pillows							
Ping-pong/pool table							
Plants, planters/flower arrangements							
Rugs							
Sheet music							
Stereo equipment (CD player, cassette deck, turntable)							
Tables							
Telephone							
Television, VCR							
Vases* (p. 44)							
Video games* (p. 36)							
Video camera, videotapes* (p. 35)							
Total							

*List in special inventory section.

Home office

Item	Description (Mfr/Brand Name & Serial/Model No.)	Purchase Date	Original Cost	Replacement Cost	Expected Life	Depreciation	Actual Cash Value
Adding machine/calculator							
Air conditioner (window)							
Awards/diplomas							
Books* (p. 34)							
Bookcases (not fastened to walls)							
Compact disks, blank disks							
Computer, monitor, keyboard, modem* (p. 42)							
Computer printer, printer supplies, paper, stand							
Computer software, games* (p. 42)							
Chairs							
Desk, accessories							
FAX machine							
Filing cabinets							
Knickknacks* (p. 44)							
Lamps							
Laptop computer, printer							
Photocopier							
Pictures, prints, wall hangings* (p. 47)							

*List in special inventory section.

Home office inventory continued on next page.

Home office, continued

Item	Description (Mfr/Brand Name & Serial/Model No.)	Purchase Date	Original Cost	Replacement Cost	Expected Life	Depreciation	Actual Cash Value
Radio							
Rugs							
Tables							
Tape recorder							
Telephone							
Typewriter							
Wastebasket							
Total							

Garage/basement/porch/deck/yard

Item	Description (Mfr/Brand Name & Serial/Model No.)	Purchase Date	Original Cost	Replacement Cost	Expected Life	Depreciation	Actual Cash Value
Auto equipment							
Benches							
Bicycles							
Cabinets							
Camping equipment (sleeping bags, tents, backpacks)							
Canned goods							
Exercise equipment* (p. 48)							
Freezer (and contents)							
Furnace, heating, central air-condition-ing equipment							
Garden equipment (lawn mower, wheel-barrow, rakes, hoes, shovels, tiller)							
Glider, gym or swing set							
Grass seed, fertilizer, bird feed							
Grill (gas/charcoal), equipment							
Hobby equipment* (p. 48)							
Holiday decorations							
Hoses/sprinklers							

*List in special inventory section.
Garage/basement/porch/deck inventory continued on next page.

Garage/basement/porch/deck 29

164

Garage/basement/porch/deck, continued

Garage/basement/porch/deck   30

Item	Description (Mfr/Brand Name & Serial/Model No.)	Purchase Date	Original Cost	Replacement Cost	Expected Life	Depreciation	Actual Cash Value
Hot tub							
Ladders							
Lawn decorations							
Lawn furniture							
Luggage							
Patio furniture							
Planters							
Snowblower							
Sports equipment* (p. 48)							
Tools* (p. 51)							
Trash cans							
Vases* (p. 44)							
Woodworking equipment							
Workbench							
Total							

*List in special inventory section.

165

Item	Description (Mfr/Brand Name & Serial/Model No.)	Purchase Date	Original Cost	Replacement Cost	Expected Life	Depreciation	Actual Cash Value
Total							

Special inventory (antiques)

Special inventory 32

Item	Description (Mfr/Brand Name & Serial/Model No.)	Purchase Date	Original Cost	Replacement Cost	Expected Life	Depreciation	Actual Cash Value
Total							

Special inventory (bed and bath linens, bedspreads, blankets, quilts)

Item	Description (Mfr/Brand Name & Serial/Model No.)	Purchase Date	Original Cost	Replacement Cost	Expected Life	Depreciation	Actual Cash Value
Total							

Special inventory (books)

Author	Title	Description (Mfr/Brand Name & Serial/Model No.)	Purchase Date	Original Cost	Replacement Cost	Expected Life	Depreciation	Actual Cash Value
Total								

Special inventory (cassette tapes, compact discs, record albums, videotapes)

Artist	Title	Description (Mfr/Brand Name & Serial/Model No.)	Purchase Date	Original Cost	Replacement Cost	Expected Life	Depreciation	Actual Cash Value
Total								

Special inventory 35

Special inventory (children's toys)

Item	Description (Mfr/Brand Name & Serial/Model No.)	Purchase Date	Original Cost	Replacement Cost	Expected Life	Depreciation	Actual Cash Value
Total							

Special inventory (clothing, children's)

Item	Description (Mfr/Brand Name & Serial/Model No.)	Purchase Date	Original Cost	Replacement Cost	Expected Life	Depreciation	Actual Cash Value
Activewear (ballet outfit, football uniform, etc.)							
Bathing suit							
Coats/jackets							
Dresses							
Hats, mittens, gloves, scarves							
Pants, slacks, shorts							
Shirts							
Shoes/boots							
Socks, stockings/tights, leggings							
Suits							
Sweaters							
Underwear and pajamas							
Total							

Special inventory (clothing, men's)

Item	Description (Mfr/Brand Name & Serial/Model No.)	Purchase Date	Original Cost	Replacement Cost	Expected Life	Depreciation	Actual Cash Value
Activewear (sweats, swimsuits, etc.)							
Belts/suspenders							
Gloves, scarves							
Handkerchiefs							
Hats							
Jackets, blazers							
Overcoats, raincoats, windbreakers							
Pajamas, robes							
Pants, slacks, jeans							
Shoes/boots							
Shorts							
Shirts/dress shirts/casual shirts							
Socks							
Suits							
Sweaters							
Ties/tie tacks/cuff links							
Underwear							
Umbrellas							
Total							

Special inventory (clothing, women's)

Item	Description (Mfr/Brand Name & Serial/Model No.)	Purchase Date	Original Cost	Replacement Cost	Expected Life	Depreciation	Actual Cash Value
Accessories							
Activewear (aerobic outfits, swimsuits)							
Belts							
Dresses							
Hats							
Jackets, blazers							
Hosiery, pantyhose, leggings, tights, socks							
Mittens, gloves							
Overcoats, raincoats, windbreakers							
Pajamas/robes							
Pants, slacks, jeans, shorts							
Scarves							
Shoes, boots							
Shirts/blouses							
Skirts							
Suits							
Sweaters							
Umbrellas							
Underwear, lingerie							

Women's clothing inventory continued on next page.

174

Special inventory (clothing, women's), continued

Special inventory   **40**

Item	Description (Mfr/Brand Name & Serial/Model No.)	Purchase Date	Original Cost	Replacement Cost	Expected Life	Depreciation	Actual Cash Value
Total							

Special inventory (clothing, other)

Item	Description (Mfr./Brand Name & Serial/Model No.)	Purchase Date	Original Cost	Replacement Cost	Expected Life	Depreciation	Actual Cash Value
Total							

Special inventory 41

Special inventory (computer hardware and software)

Special inventory 42

Item	Description (Mfr/Brand Name & Serial/Model No.)	Purchase Date	Original Cost	Replacement Cost	Expected Life	Depreciation	Actual Cash Value

Total

Special inventory (electrical appliances)

Item	Description (Mfr/Brand Name & Serial/Model/ No.)	Purchase Date	Original Cost	Replacement Cost	Expected Life	Depreciation	Actual Cash Value
Total							

Special inventory 43

Special inventory (glassware, dinnerware, flatware, cutlery, knickknacks, vases)

Item	Description (Mfr/Brand Name & Serial/Model No.)	Purchase Date	Original Cost	Replacement Cost	Expected Life	Depreciation	Actual Cash Value
Coffee set							
China							
Crystal							
Decanters							
Dishes							
Glassware							
Knickknacks							
Knives							
Napkin holders							
Punch bowl set							
Serving pieces							
Silver flatware							
Silver chest							
Stainless steel flatware							
Tea set							
Trays							
Vases							
Wine glasses							
Total							

Special inventory (jewelry)

Item	Description (Mfr/Brand Name & Serial/Model No.)	Purchase Date	Original Cost	Replacement Cost	Expected Life	Depreciation	Actual Cash Value
Bracelets/anklets							
Earrings							
Necklaces/chains							
Pins							
Rings							
Watches							
Charms							
Pendants							
Total							

Special inventory (miscellaneous)

Item	Description (Mfr/Brand Name & Serial/Model No.)	Purchase Date	Original Cost	Replacement Cost	Expected Life	Depreciation	Actual Cash Value
Built-in bookshelves							
Built-in mirrors							
Carpeting							
Linoleum/tiles/marble flooring							
Light fixtures							
Portable heaters							
Smoke alarms							
Wet bar							
Total							

Special inventory (pictures, prints, wall hangings, photo albums)

Item	Description (Mfr/Brand Name & Serial/Model No.)	Purchase Date	Original Cost	Replacement Cost	Expected Life	Depreciation	Actual Cash Value
Total							

Special inventory 47

Special inventory (sports, hobby, or exercise equipment; musical instruments, collections)

Item	Description (Mfr/Brand Name & Serial/Model No.)	Purchase Date	Original Cost	Replacement Cost	Expected Life	Depreciation	Actual Cash Value
Aerobic steps, leg weights							
Basketball equipment							
Bicycles/tricycles							
Board games, cards							
Bowling equipment							
Cameras/accessories							
Camping equipment (tents, sleeping bags)							
Collections (baseball cards, stamps, etc.)							
Crochet, knitting, or embroidery supplies							
Darkroom equipment							
Darts							
Electric trains							
Exercise equipment (rowing machine, treadmill, exercise bike, etc.)							
Fishing tackle							
Football, soccer equipment							
Golf clubs and accessories							
Guns							

Sports, hobby, or exercise equipment; musical instruments, collections inventory continued on next page.

Special inventory (sports, hobby, or exercise equipment; musical instruments, collections), continued

Item	Description (Mfr/Brand Name & Serial/Model No.)	Purchase Date	Original Cost	Replacement Cost	Expected Life	Depreciation	Actual Cash Value
Lawn games (croquet, horseshoes)							
Musical instruments							
Other hobby supplies (paint, glue, etc.)							
Ping pong and pool table							
Skates							
Skis/snowshoes							
Sleds							
Softball equipment							
Tennis, racquetball equipment							
Weight-lifting equipment							
Total							

184

Special inventory (table linens, napkin holders)

Item	Description (Mfr./Brand Name & Serial/Model No.)	Purchase Date	Original Cost	Replacement Cost	Expected Life	Depreciation	Actual Cash Value
Total							

Special inventory   50

Item	Description (Mfr/Brand Name & Serial/Model No.)	Purchase Date	Original Cost	Replacement Cost	Expected Life	Depreciation	Actual Cash Value
Auto tools							
Garden tools							
Electric tools							
Total							

www.ingramcontent.com/pod-product-compliance
Lightning Source LLC
LaVergne TN
LVHW081316060426
835509LV00015B/1535